Praise for *Bury My Clothes*

"These poems offer up a speech textured _____ construction and the complicated gorgeousness born out of survival and adaptation. These poems insist on the beauty of the darknesses we are bound by, and mean to help us live by reminding us: there is no crevice of grief or grace where something does not bloom."

—Aracelis Girmay, author of *Teeth* and *Kingdom Animalia*

"*Bury My Clothes* is the sound of language breaking open. Bonair-Agard is reaching farther both in time and in syntax to say more than he has ever said before. It is a masterwork in which the poet has found 'the canopy of night black enough for everything he's ever wanted to say.'"

—Karen Finneyfrock, author of *Ceremony for the Choking Ghost*
and young adult novel *The Sweet Revenge of Celia Door*

"*Bury My Clothes* is a gut-level read, one that you must prepare for with not only your head, but also your body. These unapologetically relentless stanzas, practically quivering with funk and resolve, will slam their fists into places you have not yet discovered. Serving up a gospel that teeters on the blade edge between calm and chaos, one of poetry's premier story-tellers has taught the city to speak with his voice."

—Patricia Smith, National Book Award finalist, author of *Shoulda Been Jimi Savannah*

"*Bury My Clothes* is a breadth of language that straddles Arouca and Chicago, hip-hop and calypso with the brawling, affirming righteousness of the Black televangelist leading us through violence and love to the wealth of unexpected tenderness."

—Earl Lovelace, author of *Is Just a Movie*

"In his profound meditation 'State of Emergency' Roger Bonair-Agard writes 'I don't know / What to think people expect anymore; / when the word black, blooms all inside / their bodies like smoke and blood; who / do they expect to walk out of this fog.' If there is a poet for this Zeitgeist, of Arab Spring, of governments toppling, a poet to listen to the people, a poet not just for this country but all countries, a poet I have been looking for my whole life, it is Roger Bonair-Agard. Part Aimé Césaire, part Hikmet, part Black Arts Movement, part hip-hop-nonstop-body-rock Brooklyn, he sees beyond borders to erase them with words. A poet of family, and funk 'ordained in the boogie,' of celebration and hallelujahs, and loss. Of knowing loss. And going on, as we all must go, Roger helps us go on, even though 'All airports now make you weep. You come / from weeping—Wednesday's child. 23. You come / from woe. Your mother and your passport tell you so.'"

—Sean Thomas Dougherty, author of *All I Ask for Is Longing*

Bury
My
Clothes

Roger Bonair-Agard

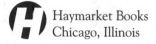
Haymarket Books
Chicago, Illinois

Published in 2013 by
Haymarket Books
PO Box 180165
Chicago, IL 60618
773-583-7884
info@haymarketbooks.org
www.haymarketbooks.org

Trade distribution:
In the US, Consortium Book Sales and Distribution, www.cbsd.com
In Canada, Publishers Group Canada, www.pgcbooks.ca
In the UK, Turnaround Publisher Services, www.turnaround-uk.com
In Australia, Palgrave Macmillan, www.palgravemacmillan.com.au
All other countries, Publishers Group Worldwide, www.pgw.com

ISBN: 978-1-60846-269-8

Cover design by Brett Neiman.

Published with the generous support of Lannan Foundation and the Wallace Global Fund.

Printed in Canada by union labor.

Library of Congress Cataloging-in-Publication data is available.

10 9 8 7 6 5 4 3 2 1

RECYCLED
Paper made from
recycled material
FSC® C103567

Contents

How I survive(d), or How I got ovah

HEART/break

Cutlass and Garlic

Postscript

For Hudley Vincent de Paul Bonair, and for the girl; coming

Foreword

*. . . the love that reassembles the fragments is stronger than the love
which took its symmetry for granted . . .*

—Derek Walcott

*Punk rock, new wave and soul,
Pop music, salsa, rock and roll,
Calypso, reggae, rhythm and blues,
Mastermix those number-one tunes.*

—MC G.L.O.B.E.

The new American poet thinks in many tongues . . .

—Meena Alexander

For one thing, *Bury My Clothes* uncovers histories, violence, rhythms, fusions,
and disjunctions that have been previously hidden in our received traditions.
For another, Roger Bonair-Agard, with his third full-length poetry collection,
is asking who and what exactly gets damned, who does the damning, how.
And of what remains, who and what are we going to call holy? All of which
brings me to two things I know about the word *calypso*: (1) the European ety-
mology of the word has a Greek root that means "to conceal" or "to hide";
(2) *calypso* shares that same etymology with the word *hell*.

In part, *Bury My Clothes* is a story of political and personal rage. It un-
covers and damns and praises not just the quintessence of rage (which is
chaotic and dull) but the story of what rage makes and what it bloody
breaks. What rage can do with and without love.

> *And if you were lucky you had some money
> left over for dress pants too because John
> was sick with a needle and thread, even
> if he did once beat his wife so badly, she had to run
> naked into the yard and we wondered why
> she couldn't just run away from a man
> with a lick-foot.* ("Back to School")

Scenes like this strobe throughout the book, complicating the speaker's moral stance and his male privilege. It is a deep examination of a young man's prolonged adolescent vanities and brutality. The insistent question for Bonair-Agard is how to become a good man.

There is no such thing as kindness and cruelty in pure form. They been grinding their hips together for so long, sometimes we can't tell one from the other. The heroes who stride through this collection are never without trouble. And it seems it is the trouble that makes them—as well as the slick music of their speech, which seems to be attuned to the music of their living.

There is the speaker's encounter with Roaring Lion, calypsonian who sang the song from which Bonair-Agard epigraphs the first section. There are the men at the bar who christen the young man into a world where rum is sacrament, where a young man learns grit, where he hones his proper bearing among elders. There is the father over the phone in the middle of a government-instituted "state of emergency" who is at risk of being picked up for being black, who can't simply say "I'm afraid," because those aren't the rules. A father of a certain stature and comportment doesn't say those things. But a poet. A poet does. As does Bonair-Agard. A poet troubles the silence.

If the father won't unknot the tie, remove the jacket, and unbutton his perfectly pressed shirt, then the son will strip down to his own black skin—in public, in America. The poet is a fool for the truth, a goddamned fool for the bare body of the truth as well as for the truth of the body. The book is a stripping down. It enacts a freedom the father does not have. There is a dimension of speech the father will not (probably cannot) test. But the speaker (who becomes a poet) will immerse himself.

Over time, of course, women are the ones to school the speaker on how to be a man. A mother, for example, who

> accosted our father at his lover's house
>
> and he tried to beat her, but rather found himself, in a fistfight;
> my mother turning over tables and lamps
>
> smashing anything she could, swinging like a woman
> insulted by even the idea of being beaten by a man

and a grandmother who "collared [her husband] in her massive stone fists // and heaved him into a corner, so my mother could not be abused."

2

We shouldn't be beguiled into thinking that the mother's lesson in manhood is just in fists, for these are the violent exceptions to an education she gives the speaker about agency, power, and the beauty of one's own dark body. She chastises a sister (or cousin) who has shaved off the speaker's hair:

> *This is when I knew black was a city*
> *whose walls were constantly under siege.*
> *This is when I knew what hymns*
> *were meant for—that they were*
> *songs of anoint for the body*
> *that was constantly at war*

> *And then my mother rose up saying:*

◆

Of course it's wooly. I have lain only with black men, men whose skin was the darkest black, men whose hair was the roughest wire and they were beautiful, and my child's hair is this way because I have never, like you, lain with anyone light skin or even remotely Chinese. And my child is beautiful, wooly, black

This book is about the way a generation passes knowledge along to the next—or how they keep knowledge to themselves. The men and women who raise the speaker from childhood to manhood belong to the same generation as Growling Tiger: "When I dead bury me clothes." The clothes are this calypsonian's style, his look. And the commerce of the Western world has made him want to own it, to make sure no one else can lay claim to it. It didn't always have to be that way. Knowledge, style, song—they all used to be passed down. But now—bury the body. Bury the clothes. Even bury what the singer and fighter can no longer wear.

Of course, Bonair-Agard was raised during the rich early days of hip-hop. And what do DJs—the grand conductors of the cosmic dance floor—teach us? The art of digging. In some ways, it's a shame we now use the word *remix* or *mashup*. The epic sets of Marley Marl, Kid Capri, the Latin Rascals, and many, many other DJs used to be called *mastermixes*, so named because of the DJs' mastery—their excellence in mixing sounds and beats

3

from different recordings, vinyl, tape, found sound, et cetera. However, those DJs were also mixing the masters: Bach, Beethoven, Brahms. This European music—called virtuosic, sophisticated, and "classical"—was also the arsenal used by critics to disparage the abundant musical invention of people of color. But if they put the masters on wax, it was the DJs who could scratch, fade, chirp, chop them into something new.

In this way Bonair-Agard's poems are an ode *and* a contradiction. The poet honors the tradition of Growling Tiger, but in redeeming and recalling it must challenge it. The DJ digs through crates and closets and basements, through trash piles—cemetery after cemetery of sound. What the world has rid itself of, condemned to obsolescence, buried, the DJ revives, reuses, remixes. This is to say, Bonair-Agard draws from so many varied sources; he samples from a variety of texts. Roger Bonair-Agard digs. You could say he unburies.

You could say he also mixes the masters. He writes in English. He makes references to Shakespeare. But the lines are enjambed against convention; Lil Wayne keeps showing up, so do signifying penguins; images of the body in making love, violence, silence, and speech abound. This is the tradition of hip-hop—to juxtapose the unlikely—but it is also the tradition of calypso. Where the steelpan was once an oil drum, it is now cut open and contains all the desire, ache, fucking, hollers, tenderness, hymns, and mischief of a people: "That quietness underneath the bamboo knocking, the steel have that too, so the steel is my master."

And steel, which was retooled to make music (and which therefore remixed its own master: oil), is part of Bonair-Agard's own remix. So whenever the masters show up in these poems, one gets the feeling they are going to get put on a platter and crosscut to new acoustics:

> The cicadas in the trees? God can't send enough
> crows to silence their plague. They've been singing
>
> since May. They know who their master is.

Is that cicada chatter a sound of terror or is it an uprising against the seasons? The seasons are their master, but the cicadas have also mastered the seasons. And they make ruckus in their mastering.

Then there is this other thing I learned about the etymology of the word *calypso*. It may also come from a French word—or it might come from a Spanish word. It's also likely it comes from a word in Efik or Hausa or Ibibio, a word—spoken, shouted, and sung during gayelle—used to urge stick-fighters on. The rhythms, call and response, and melodies that we hear in "When I Dead Bury Me Clothes" are derived from the stick-fighting circle. Growling Tiger's song is a battle cry. I don't know who the song is being sung for—the calypsonian himself? the fighter in the gayelle? or for the poet? This is significant, because the very tension of history resides inside the etymology of the word *calypso*: to conceal and unveil and urge forward and call toward. It means many things at once. Inside the history of a word for a music that is both a song and a fight, there is a history of our own submerged wonder, our most awful selves. It's a good thing, then, that the poet "knows the code" and

> *knows what*
> *it means to have six simultaneous melodies*
> *locked away forever. It is deep*
> *in the calypso, this burying*
> *of one's best clothes.*

It is good that Roger Bonair-Agard has inherited the US tradition of digging. In *Bury My Clothes* he proves, in order to reveal something of our most beautiful and banged-up selves, he is willing to go down into history time and time again—even through hell, even through a fight, and especially at the cost of singing. What follows in these pages is both the cost and the song.

Patrick Rosal
Brooklyn, New York
October 28, 2012

Preface

Bury My Clothes is a meditation on violence. It is a meditation on race. It is a meditation on the places at which they intersect, politically, culturally, and personally. This collection of poems seeks to explore the history of violence in the development of Trinidad and Tobago's steelpan culture in parallel to the history of violence in the development of America's hip-hop culture. In both thought and poem I went down the "rabbit hole" and what the poems discovered was a fundamental difference in the reasons for the creation of art in the world. Among oppressed communities of color, it is about survival. It is about establishing personhood in the world, where everything around suggests nonpersonhood. And as such, it establishes legacy in a culture and history of nonownership, through the ownership of idea and ideal. The individual's currency of personhood is only the art, and as such it must be marked as his/hers. The calypso, the new instrument, the new riff, the break beat, the graf tag must be recognized as that person's. It isn't to be handed down or memorialized in monuments. In protection of this ownership, we've made music in secret, drawn guns in beef about who stole whose rap flow. We've pulled cutlasses on other crews and stolen a prized tenor pan in the middle of the night. We've died with the secrets of wire bending and we've soaked records to remove the label, to make the break unreadable. All this while moving, changing, reinventing, and disrupting the overall cultural and artistic landscapes. Indeed, we've made ours ours, in personal style too, a tilt of hat here, an extra pleat there, a shirt open down to a navel, a massive medallion in leather or gold.

At the root of this violence is a violence done to us, and that continues to be done to us. And where this violence is real to us, where the ways in which our ability to move and live are under constant siege, so the ways in which we rebel must be constantly shifting. The art is always "next." It is always new. It is always "fresh." At the heart of this is a violence we perpetrate: against ourselves, against others, in retaliation. And at the outer reaches are the myriad personal violences of the heart, of the personal, in the quest to be eventually most fully human.

The all-time great calypsonian Growling Tiger sang, "When ah dead, bury meh clothes / ah doh want no sweet man to wear meh clothes." He wanted what made him new and fresh and a man whose personhood was established to go with him when he died. It was all he owned, all he would ever own. The refrain is a favorite rhythm in the gayelle, for the traditional stick-fights that are part of the slave rebellion history in Trinidad and Tobago. It is a song of lament and conjure. It undulates the shoulders and drives the feet into the dirt. It lifts the body up and cracks the stick. It draws the blood. It buries the man, a man, a hero on his own terms.

The poems, hopefully, do that plus offer a prayer, a signpost for a new, more total way to exist, even as they acknowledge "I am a black poet / plain and simple. I don't know if I was black before I was a poet / but I come from a people who have ways / of telling such things." The poems are about gathering again, from wherever they might come, all those people.

Dear Prologue

Two bottles of rum and the Roaring Lion

The first calypso I can remember hearing, and very shortly thereafter knowing by heart, was by a calypsonian who was already a legend in the calypso world. The Mighty Sparrow was one of the few calypsonians whose appeal had moved beyond Trinidad and the rest of the English-speaking West Indies. He had performed in England and the United States and for many dignitaries. He was adept at both social commentary and party favorites; his pen could cut both ways. Sparrow's songs illuminated—even when singing about women of ill repute—essential truths about colonial life. His wit and sarcasm were complicated by a ribald sense of humor and a daring sense of metaphor. The calypso I chose to memorize in this case could be argued to exhibit all these qualities. The chorus went:

> Drunk and disorderly; always in custody
> My friends and my family; all fed-up with me
> Drunk and disorderly; every weekend I'm in the jail
> Drunk and disorderly; nobody to stand my bail . . .

It was 1973. I was four years old.

My grandmother and mother were coheads of household; my grandmother's penchant for stern discipline was itself legend. In this Puritan household there were many infractions one did not dream of committing, but somehow I have no recollection of being censored in my loud repeated rendition of this popular song. Even my grandmother must have understood the importance of the calypsonian as griot in our midst, even as she, like many others of her generation and social station, pursued class mobility through formal education and rigorous religious indoctrination. Sparrow represented a particular generation, however, maybe the first one to benefit from the carnival arts having been raised to a level of national art and discourse. He and Lord Kitchener were the titans of the form, and following closely after them, poets like Chalkdust, Shorty, Merchant, and a host of others were providing a new vanguard. In time we would come to know soca as an entirely separate branch of the music—but we're getting ahead of ourselves.

This group of musicians was standing on the shoulders of some old high priests. These were the calypsonians who broke ground, who were champions—locally famous saga boys whose sobriquets underscored their facility with both microphone and white-handled razor: the Growling Tiger, Attilah the Hun, the Mighty Terror, Lord Invader, and of course, the Roaring Lion. These were among the earliest proponents of the form, men whose songs defined kaiso, and who, by the time I was born, were no longer taking part in the competitions, which were central to the annual Carnival celebrations. These men had defined the form. They were respected and occasionally played on the radio, but their time was past. They were the subjects of great stories by our uncles and fathers of a time we could not conceive—yeah, it was the champion stick-fighters, panmen who would as soon put a cutlass on you as talk to you, masqueraders who perfected the dragon dance and the robber speech.

And so here I was, fourteen years after my first memorized number, picking up work at the Trinidad and Tobago annual singer-songwriter music festival, a weeklong series of competitions for local songwriters in several genres. I was one of about six back-up singers who had to learn several songs over the course of the week in support of these hopeful musicians. On the last night, the festival honored the Roaring Lion with a lifetime achievement award.

I have never seen the Roaring Lion anywhere not wearing a suit, a light-colored one—usually off-white or beige, impeccably ironed—and hat to match. I remember him as a tall, slender man who moved easily and, even past seventy years old (which he already was then), was improbably smooth with the ladies. When I say that calypso sang the consciousness of the nation, when I say that folks like the Lion were legend for what they taught us of ourselves, I mean to refer you forward to the first section's epigraph, to Lion's assertion that judge, doctor, lawyer, and bishop were all occupations beneath him—that instead he would be the principal of QRC, Queen's Royal College, a boys' high school in the capital city. This is significant for reasons other than we might imagine today in a world in which teachers are denigrated and education championed only for the eventual earning power it might give. Of the three major boys' secondary schools in the city, QRC was the one traditionally seen as the black people's school. A long tradition of academic rigor and respectful questioning prevailed, and the school produced many of the country's most influential scholars, politicians, artists, and athletes. The first prime minister, Eric Williams; Nobel Prize winner Vidya Naipaul; historian and journalist C. L. R. James—the list is endless. I had recently graduated from that school and was fortunate not only to have gone there but to have known even then the importance of the legacy of men like the Roaring Lion. And the Lion knew the importance of a school like QRC.

Still, the Trinidadian ethos concerning its heroes is baffling. Maybe the country of 1.3 million is too spoiled with a relative overabundance of world-class achievers. Academic champions, Olympic champions, two Miss Universes, and two world boxing champs have all come from the small nation, and we rub shoulders on a daily basis with these heroes. We often ignore them. We take their achievements for granted.

And it is with this backdrop that on the last night of the festival, I'm leaving to go home, pulling out of a parking space, and the Roaring Lion, regally suited, with a giant trophy in his hand, is trying to flag down folks to get a lift home. I cannot believe my eyes. Lion wants a lift and people are not stopping.

I pull up next to the legend and ask him where he'd like to go. Before he gets into the car, he assures me that he only wants a drop downtown to the taxi stand, from where he'll make his way home. My mother taught me well, so I'll have none of it. I ask him where he lives, knowing full well that even if he said the other side of the island, I'd be driving him home. He says Mt. Lambert. It is completely out of my way, but I say, "Hop in. I'll carry you home . . ."

The Lion says, "Thank you, young fella," and as is my way, I speed off much too fast. Lion has other ideas though. Once we get off the street in front of the theater and turn onto French Street, the conversation goes like this:

> *whas your name sonny?*
> *Roger . . .*
> *you want a drink?*
> *well I don't have any money, sir. . .*
> *I didn't ask you if you have money, boy. I ask you if you want a*
> *drink.*

I say no more. I pull up next to Hereford's, right opposite Trinidad and Tobago Television station. We drank here throughout my high school life, and when home I still go here, often to find my Uncle Mikey on a barstool, whom I have to drive home, often at the begging request of the bar owner.

◆　◆　◆

There is a way you enter a room when you've learned the entry is important; when you know you can't leave and come back in again; when you want to be respected at first glance; when you want to leave no doubt that to fuck with you is a terrible mistake; when it is clear you are a man with rank. Any old man with enough liquor in his history knows it, even if he doesn't have it. Old men who've worked hard, with their hands, have it even when they don't know it. If you have a scar or two, if you know the business and working ends of a blade, it is bequeathed to you. Old men also know it when they see it in a youth—when the youth has learned that he is all he has; be it good joke, fist, or heft, he'd better be quick to ante up if he wants in, in this brotherhood of men.

My friends and I had been perfecting this particular brand of swagger from the time we were thirteen. We didn't know it was a thing, but we were doing it anyway. We in QRC knew who had rank; and rank could be attained in any number of ways. Sport, fight, books, jokes, women—all these things could accord a fellow rank. But only if he knows to play it effortlessly, to move, like the facility with ball on foot or sweet talk faced with a distrustful woman is native, a non-learned thing. The Lion had movement. The Lion knew entrance, and as a youth coming into Hereford's for the last few years, as a youth who knew my place in the company of grown men, I knew how to play it consequential to my years, and I knew how rank made itself manifest when I brought the Lion into the bar.

The Lion strode in. When I say strode, I mean not only is there no tentative step, I mean there is regal in the walk. I mean the man knows his place in the world, knows he must proclaim it but will not flaunt it. I mean it is the walk of a man who knows his suit is impeccable, whose knowledge and rank are affirmed. As a young man in the apprenticeship of entrances, I know not to walk directly behind him—not to kowtow, but to defer. I know to walk obliquely behind, as if presenting the magistrate. I am, as a frequent patron here, in fact presenting the Roaring Lion at Hereford's— presenting one who needs no presentation.

The Lion climbs onto the barstool at the corner of the bar, a perch from which one becomes the moderator of all bar discussion. I respectfully take a stool to his right, say a deferential good evening to the gentlemen and the barkeep, and the Lion orders a half-bottle of Vat 19. We are accorded one can of Coke as chaser. The Lion pours us our first drinks: equal parts Coke and rum in a water glass. In short order, the half-bottle of rum is done.

I have grown into what we in the Caribbean call a veteran, a man of hard liquor tastes and enough experiences to no longer be young, but not enough to yet be grizzled. That night on the barstool at Hereford's, I was in training. I was drinking with a grizzled legend—and I had to keep up, hold my liquor, and then drive him home safely and not say anything stupid in the bar or on the way to Mt. Lambert.

The Lion orders a second half-bottle of rum. In Trinidad, so much metaphor comes from the rich language associated with cricket. At the highest levels—Test cricket—the game is five days long and it's a wonderful theater. We expect our best batsmen to stay in the wicket through adversity, to bat with flair and disdain when the moment calls for it, to leave to applause. And with the Lion's introduction of this new ball, I am aware this is no one-day inning. I have to settle down and bat. Again, we are accorded a can of Coke to go with the half-bottle of rum. The drinks are progressively less brown in color and more cocoa, moving to gold. The Lion is telling stories. We learn that he has a newborn baby girl and there are tales of growing up, folks in the country, fights he has been in, and deaths he has avoided. As I'm an eighteen-year-old, the youngest fellow in the bar, my job is to lean in and laugh at the right time, speak only when spoken to and drink in time with my sponsor. Anything less is disrespect, and disrespectfulness is not just the absence of rank. It is negative rank. And then Lion says, *Roger boy, three is the luckiest of numbers*, and orders a third half-bottle.

In an inning of cricket, a batsman finds out a few things about himself. He knows, if he is patient, whether or not the pitch is playing true, whether he can expect surprises in the bounce. If he is an astute student, he knows before he is even called upon to bat whether the wicket is more solicitous of spin or pace. He knows how he must play himself into the rhythm of the pitch, how flight looks against the pavilion's backdrop, how quick the seamer is moving one way or the next. A batsman also suspects early on if he is out of his depth. If so, he stays patient. He tries to stonewall the bowlers until he can go for his strokes. With the third half-bottle I suspected I was playing out of my class. The Lion was drinking at least three times the number of years I had been alive. You do not ask out of the wicket, though. You bat and you concentrate and you make sure you don't get out. If a field sees you are in trouble, they will crowd the bat, look for you to make a mistake. You have to play the role of confident swashbuckler, even when you have no idea which way the ball will turn. And with that, the Lion says:

You good?
I good.
You sure?
Pour again, I say

And the bar erupts in laughter. Roaring Lion feigns surprise, and the bar-keep assures them:

That young fella in here all the time you know. He does come and carry his uncle home.

And the veterans and old men nod and the Lion slaps me on the back, and just like that I'm admitted into a fraternity. The old men ask where I live and where I go to school, and when I say I just graduated from QRC they nod approvingly, because to old black men that still means one of *we* boys doing something good. And one of the men says *Okay young Skipper,* which means I'm allowed back and every now and then one of the old fellas will call down a drink for me before I pile Uncle Mikey into the car. I am official now, with this nickname, even a throwaway nonspecific one. And the Lion says, *And the young fella have some throat on him, you know. He could sing.* And just like that I am knighted, right there in the bar on a stool just off the corner—given permission to make my own entrance, to make it sure, smooth, unhurried next time I come to fire a few with the fellas.

When we leave and the Roaring Lion and his trophy climb back into my car, we head to Mt. Lambert. It is four in the morning. It is an easy twenty-minute drive. I drop the Lion off in front a two-story, off-white house, and he says, *You're a good young fella. You will do well.* He strides off, suit still immaculate, hat never having left that spot on his head, tie knotted right at the throat.

Bury My Clothes

Coulda been a judge but I don't like that at all
Doctor or a lawyer but the salary too small
Bishop, but again, that's too big legal
So I became QRC principal
I became a doux-doux man, and so,
In my spare time I could sing my calypso . . .

—The Roaring Lion, "Papa Choonks"

fable toward becoming a poet

On a morning when he walked to school down the main road
across the lush botanical gardens, his top button undone
so he could hear the humming in his own chest, mimic
the mad fluster of the birds' wings, he understood himself
immediately in possession of a history he did not yet understand.
The savannah lay ahead, with its heady aromas of cut grass
and bush bug, morning sun and coconut water, and the Ben-Gay
remnants from the previous evening's matches he swore you could
still smell if you crossed the savannah walking between the goalposts.
It wasn't that he didn't know exactly what the history was. It was only
too obvious, the massive acres of savannah that used to be crop, the big
houses on one side, the opposite still, even today a massive circular
ghetto of previous barrack yards, from the tip of Belmont Circular
Road to Jerningham Avenue. It was that some days he thought he
smelled blood. And of course he would have dismissed it, as part
of the remnants from the rugby games or the hostility of a delivery
from one of the cricket matches on the unreliable and unruly wickets
placed helter skelter throughout; tiny band-aids on the savannah's
weathered face. But the blood smell was too strong in the wind, the
savannah too broad for it to be brought from somewhere without it.
Besides, he felt he could smell steel too, in that way that when the
cutlass whistles down—near, at you, or by your own hand—all your
nerves concentrate so thoroughly as to fan themselves throughout
the senses so that what is seen or heard is keenly felt, tickles the nostrils
too—and so he smelled the steel.

It was why he was always late for school, so much so that the school
began a minor investigation into the boy's habits, and his mother
wondered if the boy had taken to drugs, and grown-ups on their
way to work would report that the boy had been seen idling on his way
to school, not even hustling even though it was past seven-thirty, always
trying to look like a saga-boy, top button undone and sauntering, like
he didn't know he had a scholarship to go and try to get. But the
boy was not indolent. He was forever distracted by that wind, the
entire Caribbean archipelago it seemed assailing him from whatever

died there amongst the once-canes of the Queen's Park Savannah,
whatever still groaned under a boot-heel, so he had to sit down sometimes
with a sno-cone (extra syrup, condensed milk), just to measure the
seppy, try to figure out what ghost was calling to him from the sand track,
from the North Stand, from the Hollows where even he himself
from time to time might be able to beg a little pull-tongue and feel up
from a girl, and so he studied the bougainvillea, the hibiscus, the balisier
and dappled crocus leaf. He studied the Ti-Marie and the pond water,
the rusted band shell and the cracks in the pavement concrete that ringed
the whole rigmarole.

By the time he sat down for the first class then, of course he was tired.
Didn't matter the thermos of coffee he pulled out of his bag, he was
often asleep in less than a half hour. Didn't matter the subject either,
Latin or French, Integrated Science or Economics, his friends
had to wake him several times a day—or they didn't. He had
other worlds exploring, other histories being invented and dreamt
up. Even then, this teacher or that performing away at the front
of the room, voices still kept calling through the Main Building
jalousies—an efficient breeze coming from the Belmont barrack
yards that now housed Casablanca or Renegades—to bring
him their sermons or continue on toward the Ministry of Education in
              the west.
This is what he remembered when years later he was asked why he
couldn't stay up in class: that Africans were always bringing him
stories to tell, desperate ones, begging him for a history here,
a memory there. They would leave him with names of rivers
he couldn't understand why he knew, or the locations of lost
things. Later when he stopped writing for seven years, they would
come and take back things from him, small things, jewelry and money
to remind him how he had come to know anything at all. He was lucky
they ever came back and told him anything, insistent ancestors
they were. It meant he was always going to be late somewhere,
always hearing something nobody else heard, always catching a whiff
of something nobody had lit. He was never going to be on time
and sometimes when he was in his liquors, he left the gathered anyway,
but it meant that whenever he returned, he was always going to have
a story to tell.

A Time of Polio

My uncle Edmund had polio.
I've lived in a time
of polio. Of malaria. Of yellow fever.
Uncle Edmund was my grandfather's brother.
My grandfather loved him dearly. He looked
after him with the duty of a beloved.
This is what it means to love
in a time of epic infection, to tend
after the inflicted with the understanding
that we're all mandated to live
through massive trauma.

Uncle Edmund lived in Tunapuna.
We lived in Arouca. Sometimes
my grandmother sent me to take
food to Uncle Edmund in metal
food carriers. It was four miles away.
Sometimes I'd walk and spend
the taxi fare on beer on my way back.
I was ten. I lived in the time
of walking places. I will tell
my children this. I am forty-two.
I will probably not have any.

It is Sunday morning at a lover's
house and I am on the verge
of weeping as I say this. The food
was always still hot when I got there.
It was a tropical country. You could
walk four miles with a tray of hot
food and have it stay hot. I lived
in a time of heat. Uncle Edmund's
house smelled dank, cool. I remember
it as always dark. This might be a lie.
I unhinged the trays from the carrier,
got an enamel plate from the cupboard

and dished the food out for him so
I could take back the empty carrier. So
I could bring him food next day. I'd pour
him juice made from reconstituted oranges
and mixed with water and sugar. He talked.
The polio made it hard to understand him,
but I nodded, asked him if everything
was to his liking. I've lived
in a time of duty is what I want
to tell my children. I've lived
in a time of love. My lover

brings me the hottest, bitterest
coffee. I am grateful for this
but I am weeping for my nonchildren.
I never lingered at Uncle Edmund's,
never waited until the end of his meal.
My grandfather waited until the end
of his meals, when he went. I went
once with my grandfather. He spoke
to his brother in low, almost dulcet
tones. I'd never heard him speak
like that before. My grandfather
loved my mother dearly. She was
his adopted child, but he held us both
closer than blood. I tell you I've lived
in a time of miracles. I've lived
because of miracles and I want
to tell my children this.

That is all. That is the magic
of old age—immense loss
side by side with love. How amazing
to be Uncle Edmund, to be loved
in a time of polio and malaria
and yellow fever and dysentery.
My grandfather buried

Uncle Edmund in the family plot.
He lit candles on All Saints' Day.
I think we were the only ones
at the funeral. This is also what it means
to live in a time of polio, to be buried
unknown, but not less loved
than the pope or president. I want
to tell my children this. We are
all worried about not being good
enough for love. Imagine all we have.
Imagine all we love and live through.
Imagine what a chance we have
to endure the very worst
that might come our way.

Luck

I remember
his hands I remember
my hands the way I thought
I was a man that night
the way my mother's voice shrieked
from the other room the first time
she called for my protection

The dark had settled
into the valley of our room
when I left my brother
sleeping on the bed next to mine
and barged in my father's hands
big as a clown's that night
coming forward swinging
like scythes

A sixteen-year-old knows about loss
the myth of protecting a woman—
a sixteen-year-old   if he is lucky
has already swung his fists
with murderous intent and learned
to love the jaw those fists have cracked
He knows the heart's riot and the fear
He knows the laughing mob
of madness that entertains violence
pushes him to beg for blood—
and a boy of sixteen if he is lucky
already knows the drag of a piglet
to slaughter   the upturned plucked throat
of his grandmother's favorite cock

In the morning I remember his hands
how my own batted them aside
pushed my stepfather in the chest

—come closer to her and I'll kill you tonight—

how every sinew in me willed him
forward believing my teenage frame
ready for a grown man's weight
believing his blood my birthright

If he is lucky a boy of sixteen already knows
when to worry on danger   the blade
that might separate his flesh
from his flesh   He knows the bullet's
singing tongue   He knows the taste
of blood and the sudden sodden
crunch of bone succumbing

He knows too when to let adrenaline
hurl him forward and call it God
when to flex his stupid beautiful body
and roar   when to count coup
on the body of another and call
his own manhood to altar

A grown man if he is lucky
recognizes the boy's bluster
He gives it a dancefloor   He honors it
in his own wise capitulation
My stepfather did not break
my ribs that night   He did not throw
me from the room or knock
my teeth from my head   He did
what a lucky man knows how to do

He backs up chooses another time
listens to his own body's crumbling
narrative   He never touches that roaring
boy's mother
again

Afro

(after Kelly Norman Ellis)

My mother's afro was a magic orb
of goodness. Afro Sheen leaked
onto its ends and became emerald
in the sun. It was 1975 and my mother
told me every day that I was black; taught
me how to comb my own round globe
of halo—how to hold the pick
at its shoulder where the fist
became the bad-ass comb's
wrist.
    My mother took me
to the tailor for my first suit.
And it was super bad—light
blue, with lapels like wings.
It was sure nuf made
from something like polyester,
but the trousers bloomed outward
from the knees, so at the hems
my shoes were barely visible—
The shoes? Chocolate brown
Clarks with a rounded toe.
I was aware for the first time
that I was spectacular,
though I wasn't yet sure
what it meant to be black
in the whole world. Where
I was, I knew the light-blue
suit meant I was ordained
in the boogie. I was allowed,
even obliged to funk.
        Something
about clothes meant this;
permission and responsibility—

something about being fresh
was suddenly in play.

◆

When   My aunt
(vice principal in my elementary school)
dragged me
      from class
to
      The   Barber
my mother at work,
my head shaven
            I knew
for the first time
that my body would never
   Be
completely
            Mine.

I don't know how else
to say now what the seven-year-
old me came to know
in the bottom of my stomach.

If I'd had all the rage
         I eventually built
into a citadel;   had I
the words, I'd have
recognized
            Black.

My mother came home
saw my head and became
      A
         Bonfire.

My aunt, disgusted
said she *had* to—my head
was full of wooly stuff . . .

And this is when I knew I was black for real.
This is when I knew black was a city
whose walls were constantly under siege.
This is when I knew what hymns
were meant for—that they were
songs of anoint for the body
that was constantly at war

And then my mother rose up saying:

◆

*Of course it's wooly. I have lain only with black men, men whose skin
was the darkest black, men whose hair was the roughest wire and they
were beautiful, and my child's hair is this way because I have never, like
you, lain with anyone light skin or even remotely Chinese. And my
child is beautiful, wooly, black.*

Back to School

. . . threw on the Bally shoes and the fly green socks / stepped out the house, stopped short, oh no! / I went back in. I forgot my Kangol . . .

—Slick Rick

In the summer of '85, entering
Upper Six, last year of high school,
pants had to be gunned and pleated, narrow
—tapered at the ankles at least three
pleats either side of the fly—to be fly.

Go downtown to My Three Sons
or Jimmy Aboud's or the Long Circular Mall,
and you could cop this niceness and come
back to school with your new Ponys or Adidas
and even wearing uniforms, make your
version of the school-kit, cool.

But if you still had some country
in you, you could buy the khaki
cloth cheap, and take it to Back Street
where John, the tailor with the one
withered leg where polio ravaged him
as a child, would cut you the freshest
pants for school—enough material for
two pairs—and he'd argue with you
that he wasn't going to put three pleats in
and have your mother come back cussing him
because you know good and well your mother
don't approve of this foolishness, so he'd say
one pleat and you'd haggle for two—and haggle
to make the pants taper to sixteen inches,
not the eighteen he wanted or the fourteen
you really craved—but you got yourself

some new pants for school which you took
your time to iron and you'd sear the pants crisp
so you could look hard—the hardest hard.

And if you were lucky you had some money
left over for dress pants too because John
was sick with a needle and thread, even
if he did once beat his wife so badly she had to run
naked into the yard and we wondered why
she couldn't just run away from a man
with a lick-foot. She must like some licks
every now and then, we opined
as we strutted grinning back
to school, or gathered around boom boxes
downtown fresh dressed like a million bucks—
to discover our women, our bodies, our throbbing new world.

Lady Young Road discovery—Trinidad, 1979

our new state of mind . . .

—Chic Risque

We hairpin the narrow road
bisecting the foothills of the Northern Range
and I recognize the beat, the break
from the title track of the first LP
I owned two years earlier—a record
I played over and over in the living room
of the Winnipeg townhouse we lived in winter of '77.
I keep expecting the group
to bust in with the song *Good times*
these are the good times . . .
Instead an angry fast-talking man
kicks in the speakers of our Datsun.
You don't stop rockin to the bang bang boogie
say up jump . . .
          I shoot up from the back seat
make some wild declaration
about the foreverness of the thing coming through
the speakers. My mother rolls her eyes I think,
as my stepdad maneuvers the car around
the Queen's Park Savannah. They are still
in love. For at least one more year. Everything
is sudden and new this month past my eleventh
birthday. I've never been more sure of anything.
Will not be again for many years—*first you gotta*
bang bang . . .

Parable of Salt and Sangre Grande

morning / father

If when my grandfather (whom I called Daddy
because my mother called him that) shone shoes
on Saturday (every Saturday, every shoe in the house)
I hadn't sometimes sat on the floor in front of him
reaching into the handmade wooden box, inlaid
with shelves (one for polish of various colors,
one for polish rags and shine rags) to hand him
the various tools of this tasking when he needed
them (I was fascinated by the process of shoe-shining),
I would know nothing of the idea. the connection
between hard work and love (my grandfather
shone slow, his brow beaded up in sweat
laughing with me as we turned each
shoe up to the light to see it gleam).

And I wouldn't then see how much
my stepfather was learning how to love
(or maybe doing just what he thought was
the next thing a man should do, or
concerned with winning from my mother
what it had seemed impossible to men
from my village to win from her) when
he spoke and reasoned with me, as if
his own blood—so that I called him,
eventually, Daddy too. I went
a long time before I was willing
to accept the prayer of hard work
(wanting to believe more
in love's familiarity with magic).
But I must have known it,
must have felt the duen
of it move in my stomach early
when my own father came
from America and visited
and pleaded a kind of love

there in the yard to my mother
who stayed aloof over the balcony
(unwilling to accept his absentee
excuses), because I saw it
when my grandmother wouldn't
let him (my father) see me; and something
knotted in my stomach, because
I was inside and could see him
in the gallery pleading with her,
too, and I've never stopped calling
him Daddy, even though he never
lived in the same house with me
(it always seemed natural to call
him so).

      And maybe it's
really easy to see where this
is going now; the psychology
recognizable to any casual reader,
to anyone who took up the mantle
of loving me—
      Of course it's taken me forever
to know how to connect love
with hard work, because the work
of loving has always been like
the easy duty of shining shoes.
You can do it slow, on a weekend
morning when only you and a boy
whom you love are awake and finding
ways to make the morning glow
in a pair of old black leather brogues.

The pan tuner answers an important question about his livelihood

If the bush calls, then the bush is my master. If the sea calls, then the sea, the sand. But is neither bush nor sea calling, it's steel. I can hear every-thing in the steel; the steel can hold everything—my mother bawling and forever banding she belly, the youths them restless, and suiting women in the street, steupsing when they don't answer—the steel have all that. Plant garden? No—nothing in the bush holds noise like steel. I not plant-ing no garden. Hear that noise? Hear Mammee flip the roti on the tawa? Hear Ms. Mavis bawling behind them hardened children? Hear Gittens' hunting dogs barking? The steel have all that.

Every now and then, Daddy take the puncheon rum too serious, not often; and he come home and pelt a lash behind Mammee. Sometimes he connect and Mammee bawl out *Oh God!* Sometimes he miss and fall down and it's Mammee shouting at him *You wretch you!* And if I lean close to the double tenor, I find out the steel holding that too. So what else to do? Is where I going?

And if it's mas' you want? If what you want is the almost silent whiff a woman waist make as she wind down low, and if you want the noise of a thousand woman waist winding same time? That quietness underneath the bamboo knocking, the steel have that too, so the steel is my master.

The steel have that too.

Today's Math

The Caribs did not kill off the Arawaks
like we were taught in primary school.
The Caribs and the Arawaks managed to live
side by side for centuries before Columbus
showed up. This is today's math;
today's lesson on how to build a village
like a fortress; how your descendants survive
despite every attempt to kill you.
In the east there is a town called
Sangre Grande—big blood.
And if the Spaniards (still mad they
got so much blood of the Moors
in them) named that town
for a slaughter they suffered
at the hands of braves (see how
etymology teaches us things?)
then irony is defined by how much
white men's blood costs when measured
against the blood of those they have conquered.
Today's math is how to weave
a basket that might hold water.
Today's math is a history counted
in barrels of oil—after centuries
of sending the Indios to find gold
for Queen Isabella and chopping off
their hands if they returned without
any. And irony is the question of
gold's etymology—how far removed
from God is its brilliant shine. Almost
four hundred years later before
oil is discovered in Trinidad, and then
a mere fifty years later before oil
drums are cut and pounded
to invent the steelpan. Gold
for gold for a music that

when played well by the sons
of slaves sounds like the peal
of God's laughter itself. Irony
is the etymology of iron. And
if, as the old people say *thief from
thief make God laugh*, then today's math
is also about the Indian's tassa drums
(the ones from India, where Columbus
was actually headed when the fucker
got lost and then straight shook
by the impending mutiny). And legend says
that at Columbus' darkest hour
he sends a bird from the ship
which brings back a branch in its beak
and mustn't he have fancied himself
Noah, then: an old Jew ordained
by God to live when all around him died?
When beset all round by terror
didn't the architects of the world's
most vicious Inquisition,
which slaughtered thousands
of Jews, then turn to the lesson
of a Jew? Today's math is the etymology
of jewelry, of a search for gold
that yielded music and a gazillion
dead brown people. Big blood,
the sign reads, you are entering
Sangre Grande, and if you're lucky
enough to be a boy who gets taken
through the bush there with his
grandfather, and to see for the first
time golden cocoa pods, smelling
rich as dirt itself—cocoa the English
eventually exported back to England
so they could turn around and sell us
chocolate (that is, after their pirates'
18th-century punking of Don José

María Chacón, who, so shook
at the sight of the English armada
off the coast of Trinidad, burned
his own ships in the harbor)—then
you will wake up one morning
a man who understands the laughter
of God and why the only place
for it to come from was the deep
wailing belly of the steel drum,
and why these sons of slaves
sometimes tuned their pans in secret
so they could keep that holy
guffaw to themselves. You will
understand why Trinidadians lament
that more pans are now made in Sweden
than in Trinidad itself. You will
recognize today's math in the shiny
chrome instrument being sold back
to its maker. Irony is when slaves
become the fathers of unerasable
legacy despite their masters' fiercest
motives. Irony is the greatest
arranger of our time, Jit Samaroo, succumbing
to Alzheimer's and locking forever
in his brain thousands of pages
of sheet music. Irony is
that he is a descendant of Indians
(from India where Columbus was headed,
remember) and therefore, at least
etymologically, the hoarder of all
that gold. Spain? Well, they lost
a lot of land to American pirates,
who irony tells us have their time
coming soon enough. God is laughing
in the music of the sons of slaves
and we can see it from conquered
continent to conquered continent.

Today's math is about the perfection
of circles—the steelpan,
the turntable, what goes around
and comes around. Today's
math is how to hoard gold,
how wherever cities are built
in grids, those who build their
villages at the center of circles,
like a fortress, survive every
blooding.

The bible tells me so

and so this remarkable light, which is to say
my whole body is a sermon of shadow.

My mouth pulpits open:

Isaiah claimed that God bid him
go forth unclothed and unshod
to proclaim his word loudly. We'd call
him mad—have him arrested,
as well we should—for the audacity
to so manipulate light that we couldn't
even see his shadow. Follow me here:

Isaiah speaks chapter after chapter of a vengeful
God, a shoot-'em-up God, a God of gun-talk
and retribution and famine upon the land.

How does one call justice down
on one's own body? How does one do
the work of God in the body? You go forth
naked and shoeless of course. You trust
that what your good mind tells your hands
and your mouth and your thighs are also truths;
also your fists are God's vehicles and sometimes
your only sermon is blood.

Sometimes you eucharist from the body
of another.
She is big and tender and prostrates
before you like a last supper.

What does the body
remember at killing time? What does
the light bid us do but arrange ourselves
into ecstasy and shadow? The building

across the street is doing the Lord's
work.

Inside I've made myself a taut cord
of a body to gargoyle and sing into other bodies,
into the night, into a place of shadows and scarce
light. Say this is all God's work. Say I'm teaching
myself how to love. Say the bible is my template
for what is law and what the body says is God.

There is God in my body, and when I close
my eyes to kiss a woman, to cup her breast,
fling up my arms and enter her and we're
choired into a deep Gregorian moaning,
the building and the light and the tiny
intricacies of history's architecture all know
us and collude to call on God.

I am sure of it. This I know. I'm reaching.
The Bible tells me so.

To come from *v.* (compound/complex) —
a tentative definition

1 To originate, to elsewhere, to be
in a foreign land. To weep on your way

to the airport   2 To guilt trip, to wish
you were there for your brother's adolescence,

to miss your girl, to think of the cocoa
rich scent of her neck, her hands' sure moorings

3 To go to every summer fete in Brooklyn, to duck
bullets from drive-bys every week; return
to the same club again   4 You can almost remember

the Angel Friends' Nursing Home,
the low abandonment of your birth   5 To 40 oz

Old English and blunts in the park. To fist-fight
and gun-temple. To house-music

and broken Spanish. To one-night stand
and threaten your boss's family

6 Brooklyn is a reluctant lighthouse,
an unwelcoming harbor   7 To go home

and not be recognized. To go home
and recognize nothing. To miss

the mouths of several girls. To weep again
en route to the airport.   8 To thug up.

To slap your woman hard across the face. To come
from is to belong nowhere   9 To swing a bat

at a man's face, and belong nowhere   10 To bag up
dope, and belong nowhere. To learn to load a gun,

belong.   11 To come from is the familiar growl
of a woman's throat. To come from is her laughter

on the corner. To come from is a warehouse, is black
women singing, is all black women singing.

12 Remember to come from as song. To come
from   13 as poems, as the Arouca Presbyterian church
1974 Christmas pageant and annual talent show

14 as locker room sweat and Ben-Gay
15 Praise God from whom all blessings flow

16 You don't know any of your father's truths
and he is considering his own death   17 To come
from; clock as metronome—time as linear—verb

transitive; to come from accents both
the come, the from, is bacchic as a

drum.   18 Because you've come from
your own infant heart's evisceration and you
cannot remember being left, but you've been left
and learned how to cherish the numb of it   19 To come from

is to not need anyone. To legacy your aloneness so hard
you break   20 love   21 you break.

22 All airports now make you weep. You come
from weeping—Wednesday's child; you come

from woe. Your mother and your passport tell you so

State of Emergency

Everyone turns to look
at the nude beach in San Francisco.
Who knows what they're expecting? I want
this sun burning through this fog. I disrobe,
promptly fall
asleep.

Over the phone, from Trinidad
my father say he good—*everything like normal*
Say he *just staying home, given the curfew*
Say *is a set of foolishness. They not arresting
the big boys, the big businessmen really behind
the crime and the guns.* Say (just as I'm about
to hang up) *Acklin asked for you, you know.*
Say *the state of emergency is only to dull
the trade union momentum.* Say *is the same
thing like 1970*—which makes me scared
for him. Say *boy, only black people they picking
up. If you find 5 Indian in the 800, is plenty.*
My father is black. My father talks
some more, keeps me on the phone
when I think we're done—something
in his voice. I stay there with him,
silent, being black together.

I don't tell my love how other people
look at me sometimes—in the supermarket,
the hardware, the street, on the beach.
Who knows what they're expecting
when they say black man; what they mean
when their eyes narrow. They think I don't
see them. They think I'm all grunt
and dick. They think I stay angry.
I am. I do. I see them. They only think
they know why.

46

On the nude beach, the old man wants
to play paddleball. Says football
is too hostile. He don't even know
the half. He look at me like I'm redwood;
made of bark, like I'm already property,
like I don't have an anchor elsewhere.
He say everybody in Jamaica smokes
weed. I don't correct him on any of it.
They think they know already. They think
they own something. My clothes
are back on by now. I don't know
what to think people expect anymore
when the word *black* blooms all inside
their bodies like smoke and blood, who
they expect to walk out of this fog.

Crossroads

In the very still of night when folks are asleep
And the devil's angels fight making spirits weep
I'll be in the cemetery with horns on my head
I save a cross and two big pony invoking the dead . . .

—Mighty Sparrow, "Witch Doctor"

All he wants to know is why all his roads
have turned into rivers. Why all his spirits
have begun speaking in different unrecognizable
tongues. It's not that he's complaining
but there was a time when everywhere
the ghosts spoke in pianos. They spoke
waist music. They spoke in a pore-stippling
staccato. And now this. All this river road
and him without a way to know if to cross
or be carried downstream.

This is the moment the boy has been waiting
for. This, the canopy of night black enough
for everything he's ever wanted to say. This,
the corner, the crossroads where the magic
is right, where the voices are loudest. He calls
on the clairvoyance of women. He calls
to their skins and the wellish laughter
of their throats. He calls to the duppy
in him that unnames his own will
when it rises up to meet them. He begs
for a potion, a spell, extra time, whatever
it takes to unlock the genie in his bones.

So he consults the night. It's worked
before. He can't sleep anyway.
The night is where the answers
used to come. So many portents—
pigeons wheeling and turning—

an old calypsonian walking the streets
with a trophy in his hand—Frida
Kahlo laughing in his living room—
a duen of a woman stealing
his spirit in a foreign city—
all when the day is just black
enough to begin the song toward
blue

The greatest arranger of pan is a Indian

(for Jit Samaroo)

I walk around the room and I started to create
I know I had to prove to them, I have the ability
I decided there and then the minor should dominate
If not entirely, for most of the melody

—Lord Kitchener, "Pan in A minor"

The greatest ever arranger of pan is a Indian. This poem
is about him—Jit Samaroo of Surrey Village, Arouca
where the poet comes from; Arouca that is
Africa that is, through coastal fort, through boat,
through fire, through sugar cane, through tamboo bamboo
and the lash, through never returning to the land again,
through returning to the land again. Because the British,
because choral singing, Kyrie, through wind down low.

Jit mother play a mean dholak—everybody know
that. Jit is a Indian. Everybody know that too, and Indian
don't mess with creole people business, which is to say
not pan, not football, not rasta, not creole people children.

The poet knows all sorts of things. Right now,
he is convinced he is inside the belly of his greatest
work ever. Rum will do that.
This matters because this is Chicago, far
from Arouca, far from Jit's arrangement
of Kitchener's classic game-changer
"Pan in A minor." The poet is writing
this poem because Jit has Alzheimer's
and sometimes the poet forgets things.

Jit on guitar pan, Girlie on cowbell, Vidya
on drums, Baboolal on maracas, Sonilal

on scratcher. The Samaroo kids were
Trinidad in the broadest sense. The poet
knows the code—*I walk around the room
and I started to create*—knows what
it means to have six simultaneous melodies
locked away forever. It is deep
in the calypso, this burying
of one's best clothes. The poet
is frightened that no one will write
his songs down, now that he has failed
another woman. He knows
how this sounds—what is a woman
whom you love for anyway, but to write
your songs down.

Jit is a Indian, arranging pan. Jit sees pan
invented and killed for. This too
how we bury our clothes, make sure
no body claim what we claim. Imagine
Jit—all this music, six melodies at once
dedicated to the same arrangement. This
is what it means to be a Coolie in Nigga people
business. Hear his voice, soft like a valley
breeze, soft like a guitar pan when you wrap
your sticks right, soft like he know
he might not belong, but he know music
is all he know, music is a polyglot
beauty, music is an indentureship and Jit
indentured to these polyrhythms
in the complication of the Lopinot Valley,
the Compte de Lopinot Valley—Frenchman
who fled L'Ouverture's Haiti with 100 slaves and came
here to Arouca where the brave HyArima had already
been blooded. The Samaroo kids know
parang, which mean they know Carib Indian
and Indian Indian. They know how to resist
power, and they know how to resist family.

Jit is a Indian—the greatest arranger ever.
And he is alzheimered by
Complicatedness—his clothes buried
—for the poet ex-patriot in 1987—last carnival
before he left, buried in "Pan in A minor,"
a Kitchener tune, which is to say, a pan
tune. Hear the length of the vowels he leaves
for the wunderkind Indian, such that
arrangement, melody, arrangement, melody,
second melody during first melody. Third
melody during second melody. Fourth
melody during third—breakdown in the rhythm
section the guitar pan, the minor rising
in the way the church feared it would
so they called it the devil in music
and there was the poet child in 1987
body a whiplash to a Indian composer
looking to make love to a fat bottomed
black woman later that night, and love
is all he knows how to pronounce
but the poem is 2012 and the bar is called
Revolution, and the poet is watching film
of *Renegades*, piling melody after melody
on top itself and half expecting to see
his 18-year-old self in the crowd because he was there
and this is how black men bury their clothes
by being there, by not having to rely
on legacy, by hearing the chord change
on the film and knowing the Indian's progression
by heart and the poet could claim that they
went to the same primary school 17 years apart
but he knows the progression
because he was there, and holding a woman
who was sweating to the music the Indian man
arrange like a boss and knowing, both
of them, that there was no way he wasn't going
to win that night, before they made
love in the science building, in the chem lab

on the long bench, bruising their knees.
How you keep all that music in your head
and not have it stolen eventually? Forget
it. That's what you do. Forget Arouca.
Forget Mamie on the dholak. Forget St. Pius
Boys' Roman Catholic Primary School.
Forget the float of chord from sharp to what
might be called flat if it weren't so beautiful
and back. Bury
your clothes and the hummingbird medal
and the honorary doctorate and the thick
Indian mustache and Vidya on the drums
and Baboolal on the scratcher and Sonilal
on the guitar pan . . .

The poet is looking for himself in the film.
This is a metaphor with which the poet
is familiar. The poet is an immigrant
so he stays looking for himself
in the year of his crossing—1987,
1845, 1712. The poet claims the Indian
arranger. The Indian claims Arouca
where the poet is from. It does not
matter. Their clothes are buried. The poet
forgets things. He relies on love
to save them. Jit is locked away
in several building and piled-on
memories of melodies. All this beef
is real—and still, Jit
is the greatest. Remember for him
that his mother played a mean dholak,
that he could arrange anyone's song,
not just Kitchener's. When he's dead
bury all his clothes. Can't you see
(says the poet) fading, his memory
and faith in love giving out, finally.
Can't you see it's what he would have
wanted?

My mother asks me to take over the family's land affairs

Once, my grandfather took me to these estates.
I was clad in khakis and boots like him,
long-sleeved flannels to protect against
various burrs. He told me where to step,
how to walk so as not to surprise snakes,
what to do if one was on the path.
He broke open cocoa pods and let me suck
the sweet milk off the seeds.
He showed me how you plant
in the shade of the immortelle. We stuck
our hands in the black, wet dirt. We filled
crocus bags with doux doux mangoes,
portugal oranges, and ciquien figs.

My grandfather helped clear the land,
showed me how to use the brushing
cutlass and the crook stick; how to swing
a perfect circle in front of foot, around left
shoulder, and over the head. He showed
me where the river was, taught me
what smell was water and what was game.

Once, I could not conceive of anyone
ever wanting to hurt me. I did not consider
that the boys coming up the street
would punch me in the face
and empty my pockets.
Once, there was no way the world
was not made of nothing but pure
light. I belonged to joy and to the empty
land behind the school, and to the backyard's
red dirt. I belonged to a dark and blushing
black girl. I belonged to my strong legs

and land belonged to me as I belonged
to it.

My mother asks me to take over the family's
land affairs, and truth is, I don't want to.
I don't want this land for the price
it will exact, the family quarrels
that extend to back before I was a boy.
Too many times reminded
of whom I did not belong to.
Too many times a bastard
in the name of my grandfather's land.
I do not want this fight.

Once, when my grandfather warned us
about which of our relatives wanted
to take our land, we shushed him,
convinced in his waning years
of an encroaching senility.
No way our kin, knowing what we did
about land, about what black
people have to endure because of it,
on it, in order to have it, would
not celebrate with us the love
that brings us back to it.

Then we were told, with his body
still warm, that we weren't really
Bonairs, that the flourish at the bottom
of our deeds should account for nothing.

I've forgotten the smells and the ways
of the land, how acreage becomes
a breathing thing. I've forgotten
the simple breaking of the pods,
where to step when the river swells
and rushes. I've forgotten everything

save what good rich earth should feel like,
how it should move in the hand
and feel like your own when swizzled
in the palms.

For my grandfather, my name
remains mine, but only
the certain love of my mother
and brother will I claim. I belong
to no land and no land belongs to me.
Look at this perfect circle of sun about
my body. Look how my arms whirl
everything I own about my head.
This too is valuable. This too
is dangerous. I will do my mother's
bidding and see to the affairs
of the land. I will eat its oranges
and suck one more time from the cocoa
seeds. But this land is not for me.
It is not mine.
It never was.

The Blessed and the Blooded

Ode to my Brooklyn fitted

Brown like me—straight brimmed, you signal all my people. You, aggres-
sive white cursive against the crown—*Brooklyn*. You cock smooth to the
side over left eye, shadow like the borough—*Brooklyn*; shadow like how we
run through streets. We could call you cap—but every b-boy knows you
more than that; and when I say Brooklyn, brown, fitted, 7⅝, the whole
store knows that what I'm saying is I *stay* Brooklyn, I won't take no shit—
Brooklyn; Biggie Smalls, represent, beef patties, I fucks with Original
Ray's—*Brooklyn*; Coney Island, 9mm, A Train—*Brooklyn*. You mean to say
fist, Flatbush and gentrify—*Brooklyn*. You keep me fresh, clean, head-nod
and Sun—*Brooklyn*. You fitted, are so Brooklyn, I rock you wherever I
know you live—so you, Brooklyn, answer to where you stay at, with Oak-
land, Alaska, L.A. and Chicago's South Side. With you, I know where I
belong, that I am loved. You keep it real in Logan Square, speak low to
women in D.C. and Seattle. You preach the gospel in North Carolina. You
bold-faced, swag, bop-walked; so I can be brown, hip-hop, beautiful,
Brooklyn, bullet-proof.

Ode to the man who grabbed my arm in the bar

(for Patrick)

When you leaned in and made the decision
to grab my arm, you did not know
the cautionary tale you would become.
You'd left work earlier for a few drinks
with friends, and soon you were bar-hopping
and drunk, and happy, and a little in love.
When you finally looked up, and your boy said
yeah, Bar 13 has 2 for 1 specials
and your girl said *awesome!* you did not know
we misfits would be reading poems,
some of them terrible, but so necessary
to us that we couldn't stop even when
we knew they were bad. You did not know
how necessary you were (are)
to everything I've come to believe
and to much that I'm trying to unlearn.
You were loud, yes sir, and you were rude
and you did not know how willing I was
to forgive all this, because you did not know
you required forgiveness. You did not know
you were not allowed every right
you chose to claim and so you leaned in
drunk, to grab a man 40 pounds heavier
and 3 inches taller; and when my hand
pried itself away and made short journey
to your head, I was as surprised as you
to see you actually fall—
the slow-motion tumble of it.

You did not know when you left work
that you'd be struck down (ever).
You had not considered that
even remotely possible

and neither you nor your friend knew
how willing I became then to fight
your entire crew—even the women.
I wanted the ballet of all of you
come to me—I wanted you
to draw blood to my mouth,
to remind me how close to love-
making is the wrestle, have me
believe in gladiators, gargoyles
and the night again.

Small man, you could not know
that I cried after I hit you
that I've always wished myself
beyond the tribe of blood, dirt
and immediate consequence—
but you, you brought me back—
you thought you could put your hands
on anyone you felt like, and I
had to remind you otherwise,
as I slipped out the back door,
to avoid the cops, who surely
would see it your way,
and take my chance instead
with my body, my fists,
my good two legs running,
knowing I could trust only
my hands' self-made laws,
the shadows the buildings make
of the city—the night
for me to hide in.

Ode to the man who leaned out the truck to call me nigger

Before I met you that night, before you leaned out
the truck window to call me nigger, I knew
nothing of my own flesh's surrender
to blood, dust. But I did know speed; I knew
the weight of lumber and the forearm's debt
to torque. I knew (and loved) the sound of shatter-
ing glass, the quick snap of a duressed jaw.
I knew the taste of my own blood. I'd had
a fist test the tension of my kneecaps,
my heart's tight buckle.

What you taught me as I leaned out
the window, New York speeding by
at 50mph, to catch you,
was about the song of the air
at night, how—as I braced my foot
against the dash and limboed out
to swing at your windscreen—I craved
the timpani of glass and metal
the soprano of your screams.

So easily I could have fallen
under your truck's wheels. I was
in search of love and somehow
knew you had it to give in blood,
which I needed to husband
my quiet, quiet rage. I had
not thought then about how I wanted
my body disposed, that I loved
a woman to call me names in bed.
I wanted a song that was mine,
something to belong to, a love
I'd recognize when I heard
my true name sung
in the street.

Ode to my headphones

You anoint me youth-culture, black,
blank gaze and swift to fist; my head
in the vise of your grip, under
this hoodie, I become twenty years
younger: a stick-up kid, a flight risk.

Because I look like a runway signaler,
a crazy tarmac matador, my hands
slashing the air as you bulge from my temples,
I stay in flight. Just short of a helmet,
unleashing a steady assault of bass
directly to my heart, you stay
defibrillator, dance instructor, hypnotist
and hip-twister.

You deliver me Fela and Kanye,
Marley and Sparrow, Black Stalin
and the Wu Tang Clan, Nina,
Rudder, Amy Winehouse, Beres Hammond,
Ice Cube, Mikkey Halsted, permission
to talk loud, my mother's vicarious
wishes of dance—you
godfather my hip-hop and my dance
hall, in every head-nod and stutter step—
I lose myself in my footfalls'
own beats—you guardian
of the long-distance train ride,
the long-distance run,
the long-distance dream
of black boys everywhere.

Ode to basement bangra

The tassa is heavy with water.
Its *doon-doon* is deep as the Indian
Ocean. The tabla is a ruckus of
.celebration. Such a paganism; such
beauty that ignores the convention
of space on a dance floor. The turbaned men,
the heavily jeweled women, dancing hands
gesticulating to a confusion of percussions,
to come down to earth heavy in the hips
on the African downbeat rooting us all.
The drum machine is a hypnosis, heavy
with bones—the guitar licks wide
as the Atlantic. Such a gospel that marries
these hips and thighs to the dust rising,
the wail of the left-behind. So much dougla
on this dance floor. The bellies are a ripple
of alphabets. The DJ can almost not fuck this
up—all these fists, all these ecstatic feet
the sweat so thick, the floorboards are a mystery
of mud, the exits aflame with heat.

Ode to the hunting knife

Your scabbard is the laughter
of any man who once lived
on the big end of surprise.
You sound like a violin
    when drawn swift—blade
    singing a soft death
    against the leather as it births
    toward the light   and then

your sweet weight,
like a small cantaloupe
or a large avocado—the heft
complete

When I roll my fist around
your handle, four fingers nestle
the hilt's grooves like piglets
against the sow's underside.

Spine against my forearm
I become   weapon;
my hands   beams of light—
my whole body dances
musicked by your handle's
    intricate carvings

our love
    is close—our history
deep.
    Sometimes it is your song
I want again   your kiss
against my skin
        the blood-letting

sweet

Ode to the cutlass/machete

Oh grooved flat-side blade, heavy
and stinging to plan-ass a wayward
man. Oh cutlass, Oh machete singing
with the weight of the sugar cane's
yellow stalk. No one fears your sharp
edge. You are no more than garden
tool. You are protector and family
friend. You are perfect balance.
You are government of the forearm's
striations. You are a sailor dance and
a saga boy's pirate walk, a masquerader
unafraid of his own powder.

Oh brilliant machete, snatching at light
from the sun, calling out tune
as you whistle down, blood seeker
in the fist of rage. We garlic your edge
for the unhealable wound, salt it
for the unforgivable sting, but no one
is afraid of you. You are made for the edges
of lawns, for the slow amelioration
of the loamy earth. You sleep under
my pillow, leaned against a door jamb.

Nothing but torque, steel and cedar,
your voice is an echo when bent right,
when the threat is dragged
across concrete, a stick-fighter's song reborn,
a memory retained in the broad scar
across a pan man's black back.

The Black Album

Word of my coming—an ars poetica

(after Cornelius Eady and Joy Harjo)

I am a black poet—plain and simple
black first. I do not know
if I am a poet before I am a man
or a man before I am a poet.

I come from a people who have
ways of telling such things.

I come from a people
whose history is inside history.

Someday,
there will be a great tale told

of how 500 blackbirds fell out of the sky
the day I discovered this.

I live in an age of bodies
declaring themselves to heaven.

Sometimes these bodies fall
from the air—sometimes wrap themselves
in shrapnel—other times they press
the backs of their heads into speeding bullets.

None of these ways will claim
me. I am confident
of this.

My song has always been heard.
There is a drum in my throat.

I was black before
I was a boy.

There is record of this
in the air over the fire which consumed
a Brooklyn nursing home.

I come from a people
who remember such things

who tell stories inside
the stories we are told. We are told
we are not a people of history
but I am a black poet
so I know better.

I've been there for the beginnings
of things, so I know better.
I was coming over a mountaintop
in Trinidad when hip-hop was born
so I know better.

My people tell several stories
about the supernatural. My grandmother
was once threatened by a ball
of fire in a coconut tree. I believe
her story. It might have been word
of my coming.

The lagahoo dragged its chains
around our yard. A woman whispered
an unholy magic on our steps
and my grandmother's foot swelled
to the size of a tree trunk,

a woman whispered an unholy magic
into a bowl of cucumbers
and my grandfather fell
deathly ill.

My grandmother survived.

My grandfather survived.
My mother survived.
I survived. This is how
I know the birds flinging
themselves onto rooftops have
something to say. This is how
I know I will not die by bullet
or fire—how I know
I am a black poet.

My great-great-uncle Obidiah was hobbled
for running. He ran as a way
of spell-casting. He bit a man's
ear clean off. This is also
a way of casting spells.

This is how he protects me,
how I know I will outrun
every bullet. My mother
insisted on my blackness.

My mother left me in a foreign country.
She came back for me.
She came back for me.
She came back to save me
to tell me how black
I am—because the sky
rains finches and jackdaws
in tribute to me
because the sea sings up
its carp and catfish, its crabs
and salmon to proclaim me

man, poet, boy, black, magic,
god, god, god, god,
poet, black, black, black,
black,
unkillable

*In 2010, an entirely black penguin was discovered in Antarctica.
The genetic possibility of an all-black or all-white penguin is only
minuscule. The following is taken verbatim from a Reuters news
report covering the discovery:*

*"An all-black penguin has been discovered in Antarctica. It seems
to be
assimilating nicely and has even found itself a black & white mate . . .
Recently discovered all-black penguin seems unafraid to defy
convention . . . .
Biologists say that the animal has lost control of its pigmentation.
Other than [that] the animal appears to be perfectly healthy. 'Look
at the size of those legs,' said one scientist. 'It's an absolute monster.'"*

The all-black penguin speaks

17 facts you did not know about me

1. I was born here, raised here, met my mate and warmed my
    eggs—here.
2. Fully ten seasons passed before you noticed me. Don't make up
    theories now,
Johnny-come-lately.
3. Penguins are color blind.
4. Fuck your bell curve, motherfucker—I know that's not a
    fact. It's an imperative.
5. Penguins deliberately don't read so we wouldn't have to learn
    words like *assimilate*, like *discriminate*, like *mutate*.
6. We pray every day. It's a simple chant:
    Evolve, Evolve, Evolve
7. Can't you see it's getting warmer? Don't you see the ice melting?
8. I know the word *rhetorical*, bitch

9. I'm actually the same size as all the other penguins.
10. You suffer from *ocular negrophobia*, the condition in which all
    black (all-black?) things look really large and scary. Yes, I
    know that's a fact about you, motherfucker.
11. I hate you.
12. I don't believe in the same God as you.
13. Evolve, Evolve, Evolve
14. There are two other all-blacks. We do not know each other.
15. I'm prettier than you.
16. I'm making up a song about you. It's called "Albino Mother-
    fucker."
17. We have a few all-white penguins here. We're cool. They hate
    you too.

Infinite blackness

(for Saeed)

This is not
    a threat
not a way to say we plan
on blood—no one ever
plans on blood—yet
blood comes—and when
blood comes, blood
    moves   hard

You know how sometimes
the clouds pass over a full moon
and it looks like the moon
is moving—real fast,
    that's how blood moves—unmoving

and suddenly full—this
is no threat—this
is a love trumpet   You
have created infinite blackness
which now you have
    no idea how to contain   You

one-drop defined whiteness' purity
and now we have niggas who look
like you, among you   Isn't
    that   amazing
how solidarity gets made—
how niggas find other niggas
to get up with?
In South Africa there are gangs
of black boys who umbrella
themselves under two major
banners—the Biggies and

74

the Tupacs   we have niggas

          there—halfway round
the globe—ready to ride
right now. You don't really
want us calling on those armies,
do you Mr. Limbaugh,
Ms. Palin, all you bankers who took
the money and booked

In Jamaica there are gangs
of black boys who umbrella
themselves under two major
banners—Gully and Gaza
You see what I'm getting at
don't you, Mr. Santorum,
Arizona, governor of Wisconsin?

Niggas know
          the connection amongst niggas.
We aren't sitting around smoking crack
and drinking malt liquor. We know
the connection between Alabama's
immigration laws and NBA owners'
attempts to sucker punch the players—
that's a lot of niggas—
                    just waiting

I'm telling you this Ms. Bachman,
Mr. Gingrich, because I love you
and it appears neither of us is going
anywhere—all you jail builders
and school closers—there are

niggas in Hiroshima, Palestine
and Des Moines—just waiting
for the call. There are church

niggas and transgender niggas—
in the cut pretending to not pass
notes, Mr. Pfizer, Mr. Monsanto. We

see a clear through line from Emmett
Till to Trayvon Martin, and we've been
memorizing the names of every nigga
you killed, whose names you kept
out the papers. We're here and we know
what's up and we've been memorizing

the sound of whistling in shell casings.
Take heed—not with guns—look
for once at yourself. Imagine
today what the fuck you look like
in all your Columbus Day whiteness.

We are invisible but we see—we
are infinite—niggas are indeed
in Paris, Mumbai and Brooklyn.
We are not just making rap videos
and we ain't whistling Dixie. We

bridge builders over the world's
most troubled waters and our
tools and numbers are endless
and we gather at your skin
        like blood. We locust. We

love, and we have begun
to move. Consider Harriet Tubman,
Nat Turner, Denmark Vesey, Marcus Garvey,
Shirley Chisholm and Malcolm X
as prophecy.   It is possible

still, Pope Benedict, George
Zimmerman, Bush American

Dynasty, to save yourselves
simply by learning how to act
right in company, by reading

Baldwin and hooks, Ralph
Ellison and Audre Lorde
by listening to Donny Hathaway
and boys beating buckets
in the subway.   They/

we have things to say. We
are worth your time. We
love you—lean in—this
could save your life.

On asking a black woman
if you might touch her hair

Be Black

If you aren't black, be her man,
or a friend since childhood.

Preface the request with *I know this
is weird and calls to mind many
crazily embedded racial histories
but* . . .

If her hair is dreaded
rethink the request.

Preface the request
with the honorific "Sister"
only if you are black.

Be Black

Make sure you've seen
her smile first. Make sure
you know what kind of day
she's been having.

Make sure you're the only
two people in the room.

Have a well thought out
response for when she asks
why.

The word *fascination* should not
be a part of the response

especially if you are not Black.

Be Black

Have more than one
black friend.

Do not bring up how much
you know about black culture.

Be Black

If she doesn't answer you
do not assume she didn't
hear you
        the first time.

Fade to Black

Grow like a fetus with no hands and feet to complete us
and we return like Jesus, when the whole world need us

—RZA (Wu-Tang's "Reunited")

Shonettia says she has two tongues
and I, of course, reply *I know.*
And she assures me this is no metaphor,
there is another tongue in her mouth
behind the obvious one, down in the throat,
so to speak. When I ask to see it, she says
it isn't yet time, I'd always known

of the second tongue. Truth is,
there is nothing to report.
Angel and I are forever *investigating*
Blackness—from the dungeons of our own skins,
our sociocultural high horses
(she back East in a college I used to attend,
I in a Midwest she couldn't escape fast enough),
we know black women stay double-
tongued, *stay* in the cut of waiting for the right
time to tell the truth.

The last season of the *Arsenio Hall Show*
gets buckwild. Arsenio, no doubt black,
and front man of the only such late night talk
show, has already catapulted Bill Clinton
to the presidency, already interviewed NWA,
let them say *nigga* on air in prime time, let them explain
themselves in the song "Fuck the Police." Arsenio
has had Eddie Murphy and Michael Jackson
present each other with awards. Arsenio has
invented the dawg pound (and birthed a whole
new generation of frat boys in the process—you
have no idea how black this is). Arsenio has punked

Vanilla Ice. Here's the blackest question ever asked
on late night television on any major network:

Ice,
why are you out in public with Flavor Flav these days?
Are you trying to show us you have black friends?

Arsenio dug deep into the dungeon of his own
high-top fade and purple suits and got real black
for America; so black, he let Farrakhan explain
himself, so black, he showed us Mike Tyson's
human face—*you have no idea how black*
that is—so black, he lined up an all-star cast
of rappers to close out the last show of his last
season, some would say, his career.

Harriet Tubman—double-tongued
Audre Lorde—double-tongued
bell hooks—double-tongued
Angela Jackson—double-tongued
Marian Anderson—hella double-tongued
Odetta—double-tongued
Phyllis Wheatley—double-tongued

Oprah Winfrey is about to run
the cultural end-around of a lifetime,
about to get so black, *how black?*
so black you'll fuck around and sit on her
at the movies; oil spill black, Strom Thurmond
grandchildren black, Flava Flav and ODB type
black. I'm rooting for Oprah's
second tongue.

Shonettia says she has less control
of the second tongue. It will not speak
alone. It cannot make love. She can make
it cough, she says, or make beautiful
epiglottal noises that sound

like they come from her heart. Even these
she will not yet exhibit. Angel says
she stays bored with professors
who've done less investigating than she,
says the least black thing going is Finals Week,
says she's getting words tattooed up her shoulders
that'll burst into unrecognizable birds—says this
is the blackest thing she can think.

We're steady convinced we're post-race,
while the first black president fields more death
threats than the previous forty-three combined.

Fifteen years ago, Arsenio's last show fades
to black with a glossy onyx stage, peopled
by a who's who of rap literati. Only one voice
can be heard above the fray. It's
Ol' Dirty Bastard, telling a truth America still
isn't ready for—a truth Arsenio had no business
revealing:

The black man is God
The black man is God
The black man is God
The black man is God
The black man is God

Shonettia could have schooled him.
It isn't yet—*time*

luck and the dark

how can i move the crowd
first of all, ain't no mistakes allowed

—Rakim

At Cozine and Van Siclen they set
on me like a wolfpack,
a shark-school.
I was 19. I was fast.
I was afraid.
I liked dangerous
        places, like crack
alleys and Harlem and the bedrooms
        of older women.

Like piranhas on a piglet,
they came for blood.
They came
        for money. They were *wilding*.
It was 1987. I was about
        to be a casualty,
a statistic.

I was slender. My fists,
blocks of warm wood. I tried to talk
my way out. They set on me
like *motherfuckers*. They were thick
as squad cars, tall
as the projects. They talked
slow and gold-toothed.

They set
on me so I
watched the angles.
I watched the
streetlamp.

I
    watched the moon.
  They were
swarming, dark
    as shadows under train tracks.
They were dark like
    rap music.
They were
    coming out of cars.
I watched
  the moon   glint
off a fire hydrant.
I watched
the space between
the garbage can and chain
that corralled it to the light post.
I was planning to run

like Harriet, like Frederick Douglass,
like Tommie Smith and
John Carlos like Mexico '68
and the American
flames
    that followed
like Deion Sanders at the Rose Bowl
telling the other team's bench
he was about
    to take the kick-off back.
        I was about
to take the kick-off back,
but they were fat medallions,
four-finger rings,
  I was 19, one month
deep in East New York,
Brooklyn. I was tight
  khakis and a floppy hat.
They were

Levis and pistol whippings,
showing off
    handles
        of guns. They shut
the corner down. They turned
off the lights.

&&&&&&

So what it is nigga
my hand hits
    his chest—sound
is bass   is flatness
a broken woofer   sweet
music. I run
like a round from a Ruger,
like ninja smoke,
like *grab that fool!*

I run. I know
someone's raising
a nine to my back
right now. I'm technically sound.
I'm gifted. I'm incapable
of ever being caught ever.

East New York. I run
like night I'm   ghost
sound depends
        on me
        for morning.

The all-black penguin explains some things to Jonathan Livingston Seagull

Look, I'm not you. Don't really have that type constitution; that time to fuck with time, you feel me? Even though some days it seems that's all that ever happens. I love how fools show up when you full grown and act like they made you themselves. Been really looking for ways to keep my head down and stay invisible. It's enough that I'm someone else's trick of light, some jealous god's plaything to be experimented with. Trust me, all I want is a quiet life with a river to cross in the end. Nobody ever told me I was different, but you can't draw all the heat without asking yourself sometimes why you got left in the kitchen; know what I mean? I get you. I really do. At some point, you just want to go so *clear*, they can't tell you shit no more about nothing so simple as the feathers on your back. There's no secret here. I was born—exactly *this* black. I've shined like a target from the moment I cracked the shell. So I wasn't surprised when they finally came with their measurements and their helicopters and their cruise ships. You might've got it right—move so fast, you transcend the captivity of time and space. Now ain't that something? Be black and that's all you ever have time to learn to do. Sometimes no amount of work can levitate you past how brilliant you gotta shine. Ask the Hotten-tot. Ask Caster. Ask Muhammad Ali. Ask James Brown. Ask any nigga who found a way to make a dollar out of fifteen cents.

because everyone wants to know what's next

The edge of blackness must not be confused
with the edges of physical things—blades,
buildings, tables, saucers. Rather
this edge is horizon, constantly moving.
The edge of blackness is gray, is sunrise,
is emergence and exorbitant
dis-appearing. For instance, where
blues becomes rock and roll; where
blues becomes punk; where blues
becomes jazz; where blues is the song
everything makes when it's missing
where black takes itself to a point
of exhaustion and rather than fall off
engages the process of re-becoming.
The edge of blackness is not edge
at all. It is rebirth, even when rebirth
is co-optation, even when rebirth is recast
—the edge of black   stays black,
even when costumed   where blues
becomes funk, where funk becomes
rap, where we know black by the way
black walks, or attacks the basket
or takes the yoke and makes of it
medallion, where the edge of black
lives and the edges of black live
a constant state of be-coming.
Check it—the more what isn't black
to contain the borders of black, bleed
and sunrise and wail and make new
ways to make a horn sound like a hungry
child, a retreating wife, a gun barrel's
slither, a daffodil opening in a bottle-
strewn lot.
    The edge of blackness
is a religion whose heaven promises

that drums become feet and whole
languages hieroglyph into gang signs.
This is how a religion signifies
deliverance, signifies the edge
is constantly moving—that the neighborhood
of black can be read one moment in
a black boy's sagging pants,
a fat woman's hot comb; needs
measurables and formula to speak
to blackness' edge, when black
only needs the cover of night—scratch
that. Black needs its own memory
of borderlessness, a train whistle,
ship dock and field uprise. Think storefront
church, underground railroad and juke
joint. Exactly, edge covers itself in nothing
but night. The next anything is to miss
the point, the journey
of transformation, busy after "empirical"
and "evidence." Whole civilizations' song
missed searching for these unreliable
vehicles. Whole poems fucked up
trying to answer the question,
rather than just be
the fade. Still, here's the obligatory
nigga to misdirect the be-ing of black-
ness' becoming blues becomes jazz,
becomes rock and roll becomes funk
becomes rap becomes universe and
black
becomes

How I survive(d),
   or How I got ovah

learning to read

(after Frank X Walker)

Because my mother never shooed me
from the room when she was talking
about politics, and never thought
I should leave even when the sweet
gossip about a friend was on tap.
Because my mother let me join
in when adults spoke and never
spoke to me in a babyish
condescending tone—Because
my mother drank good whiskey
and played cards and let me sit
there and laugh when she threw
the King down hard on the table
and talked shit to the men, I knew
that when she said, *Roger,*
this is for big people, that the grown-
ups were talking about fucking.
Because my mother's perfect
diction (which kept most things
audible, even in sotto voce) slid
then into a buttery whispered song;
because my mother's voice got smoky,
low, and conspiratorial, I giggled
alone to myself, even when I couldn't
make out what was being said.
And because I got then to spend
hours in the study alone
with books that were also for big people;
and read at length
about exactly what my mother
spoke in her smoke and whiskey
voice, I never tried to peek my head
out early and back into the conversation.

I was learning the silky goodness
of the forbidden word: how a woman's
barely visible slip spoke a rustled
language against a thigh, at what angle
the cocked cigarette meant a blade
was hidden, and at what angle, a wish.
My mother taught me through the genius
of banishment and access all at once
that language was a joy to share
to withhold, a power to wield—
whether the language was her deep
resonant call for me to come in
from the streets at twilight, a measured
question about my studies, or alone
amongst books, the gradual knowing
that a woman's legs, in the crossing,
spoke gunshot, refusal, heat.

Recall (i) the History of Church Music

The song rose from the gut of morning
all the way to the rafters of noon—song of praise;
song of protection, congregants bugled the tiny church
aloft. Some said it was the only way
the building stayed steady, betrayed its crumbling
plaster and termite-ridden beams. The reverends' job
easy in the countenance of such faith, wade
in the water of the people's song, prayers
of the elders and the children. Preach sum
of the village gossip and the nicknames of local legends.
Enough existed in the valley out of which to make music
to God. All they'd need was a preacher with a dance
in his voice; a child without shame,
to sing in Jesus' name.

list of demands

(after Evie Shockley)

> *now i'm in the limelight / cause i rhyme tight*
> *time to get paid / blow up like the World Trade . . .*
> —Notorious B.I.G.

Give me

    the perfect
        circle of your voice
  40 acres   and a recording studio

  my name back   the perfect weave
  the land on which i work
  children who will believe me

  my religion back   a good grave   blues music
  fair dollar value

  the moon
  Nat Turner's confession

  the sound of my voice   the perfect split of the red sea
  that i am not crazy
  a right to believe

  my son's right mind
  my daughter's perfect dreaming

  Billie's gardenia

  a believable tomorrow
  a new car   sturdy shoes
  a mule   a musket   a circus
  every shade of black

my whipped back   my grandmother's huckster hands
my grandfather's blazing speed
my father's pride

Malcolm's changed mind

a footrace to the sea

liberty/

death

Recall (ii) Word made Voice

The child was born out of wedlock
Naturally.
The child came from another land
Of course.
The child's lungs were larger than
Wolves.
The child's limbs would not walk
They Shiva.
The child sang and sang
and sang
He played the drums with the bone
of his body.

His hands learned the wand of flourish
He stamped his feet when he spoke

Everyone listened.
No one heard a thing.

The Night Biggie Died

*(live from Bedford-Stuyvesant, the livest one, representing BK to
the fullest . . .)*

—Notorious B.I.G

The night Biggie died I
28 dreadlocked
   taut on fire
    175lbs I fast
and angry and in love

    kissing a woman
and then   another
   her tongue was incandescent and Biggie
was *Notorious*

I squared off with some dude
"Who Shot Ya?" blared
out the speakers   baggy blue-jeans
and tongue-loose boots   I barked
I threw
     my hips into a deep far corner
     of the bass groove

I buried 20 dollars in the juke
Biggie nodded to the beat on Wilshire
Puff was at the wheel Suge Knight
   in jail   my tongue
in the mouth of a woman
Clinton was president
George W Bush   coked up
Biggie   promenaded Wilshire

my torso   a roll
of wire   my fists

97

stones The night Biggie died
I rode the back seat
   between two women   I groped
their thighs   they were leaning
over the edge of my cavernous need
their bodies   taut lassoes
their nipples hard as ammunition
      The radio crackled   we left
the bar   the backseat stank
      sweat as Biggie royal waved down Wilshire

I lied   to get both women
into my dorm   I pretended
they both had my whole story
   I loved them dearly

I hadn't learned how
   to say *No*   the night
shots squealed on Wilshire

     Earlier we'd stopped to eat
I blessed my food
   black olive omelet
  made the sign
of the cross

   Wherever we live   God is
Biggie   being rushed to hospital

Wherever we fight God is
   who knows the science
of the head-nod like   a bullet
in wait   Biggie   a black sieve

the light of God moves through us
   my tongue in the mouth of a woman

Wherever we die God

returns   Biggie
and a choir of sirens
        on his way

the love of God enraptures
    she squeezed me frantic
under the table

Biggie's farewell
    the Brooklyn illest   *Unbelievable*

the power of God protects us
We made a raucous hosanna
        of our bodies that night

we sat in the car stunned
when we heard the news We didn't know
if to cry Biggie   shot
in Los Angeles   I made a grave
of a woman   New York held us
all in our public
    weeping our eyes leaked
blood   our son Biggie dying
on the streets of Los Angeles I dying
in the bed of a woman or she dying
    in mine   Love went to war
in both our hearts   this is the music
I became a man for   This is the second
line funeral I danced to
as Biggie lay   I   born
of the juke
    I love it when they call me Big Poppa

You should have heard the women
moan for Biggie that night   You should have
heard the ropes' rough ripping as we lowered
our caskets   into graves

Recall (iii) Wolves

My first pan was not made from an oil drum like the grown-ups' pans
were. We had practice pans made from tin, painted gaudy red. I learned
that year's calypso on it before I had to be taught. I invented my own
arrangement. taught it to everyone. I played a single tenor. I was seven. I
cannot remember any of the notes, but I remember my body swaying be-
hind the pan when I played the hymns.

My hands were an intricate kata.

I remember that.

I remember the ripe adolescent sweat of the director's
daughter.

the baby powder on her neck. I invented my own
arrangements of things: hymns, arias, calypsos. my becom-
ing.

My first pan made a silly descant of a noise, but I beat it into swing. I beat
it into ghost. I beat it into a story I could believe.

Here's the first chapter: once upon a time there was a boy. He was afraid
of nothing. He believed himself invincible.

This was not remarkable in the way of boys, but when
he opened his mouth; when he sang, everyone knew—his lungs
were made of wolves.

Meditating on Lil Wayne, or
How Weezy met Billie Holiday

(on craft in poetry) well craft is . . . like magic really
that's why they call it witchcraft right?

—Li-Young Lee

you sprite-limbed rhyme-sayer
you conscience America young brother—
lazy hip-gun bling-grinning crawler
you an angel niggah
    Believe that!
your body Picassoed up with love
   and dead homies
you internal-rhyme grimy
    fantastical master of obscure allusion

you reincarnate Billie Holiday's
    gravel magic you make
       black music mystical rage
in the ghost of her
             throat

you Pied Piper lunatic emcee
rhyming   Your craft is magic
the children follow you
to the cliff and fly back to Africa
you microphone Merlin   Hendrixing
the national ethos like a muthafucka

you tattoo Billie's collapsed
veins on your throat

Imagine you tap them like maple trees

Imagine how fast you solve America

Imagine Oprah in love with you

Imagine a studio full of gardenias
    cigar smoke and Southern Comfort

Fuck parental advisories

Fuck the Reverend Calvin Butts

Imagine what the break beat
    beats back from Billie's bassed rasp
what your throat do
    with all that strange fruit

How I learned to talk, or Why I will not be killed; a warning—ars poetica

It is a living vibration
rooted deep within my Caribbean belly
Lyrics to make a politician cringe,
or turn a woman's body into jelly . . .

—David Rudder

I'm trying to tell you what I know of poetry:
how I learned to talk, and how there was
always a stage involved. I'm trying
to tell you even now there is a throbbing
behind this keyboard, my body davening
to something it thinks it hears. The root
of this so far planted, it knows nourishment
in the spine's call, wants what rushes up
the back to call me to move, its
messiah on Earth—its high priest
of making meaning the body's
insistence it live. If I tell
you this is a language only translatable
as drum, you will say you have heard
this before, which is to say you know
nothing of how the center bass thump
squats the body, pushes up
and comes brawling its way
into my throat; wants to fill
stadiums because it remembers how
many things have tried to kill it.
It remembers the sea, smell of blood.
It makes my mouth full
of *mornin loves* and *kiskidees*—words
that only begin to say what seethes
inside what I'm dying to have you know:
everything about the desperate,
uncuttable umbilical to old old old

black women who still say *Son*
who get up and hold me when they hear
Rudder or Lion or Sparrow or Chalkie
and they don't care that I'm crying;
loss is unnamable except we have
a music snatched from gods and roots
the insides of oil drums; it's concerned
to make communion with the shackle
and the bottom of the sea and iron
in a dirt that most of us will never see
again. I'm telling you these psalms
are called Calypso; they are
spells to Shango, they supplicate
Osun, they hold in the hollow
of bamboo, cut and dragged from
off the St. Ann's Hill, the ring of Ogun's
forgings toward war, the confusion
of *I want to go home* and *I will not*
work this land and *hibiscus* and
woman I don't know how to tell
you, you are my earth and anchor
This is how I learned
to talk. This talk, this calypso
the warp and weft of what it means
to be black and remember, in the way
only blood in the spine remembers
the dirt in that continent we still
taste biling in our throats
when we weep, the lyrics to the song
of the cutlass ringing against the steelpan
stansion, the morse code of a scar,
the secret of the dragon's dance
in the masquerade and the stories
still impelled by the sea and manifest
as bodies killed and discarded in cane fields.
also, how many columns of old
women and brothers and uncles

whose vocabularies are built of the same
passage of blood, who know us when we sing
and the *d-doom* of the drum signals
other words learned by my spine like
bury and God and *soca* and *wine*
down low and *we're not ready*
to die today, we're not ready
to die today

HEART/

break

Hip-hop started out in the heart
Now everybody tryna spark
Come on baby baby,
Come on baby baby
Come on baby baby
Come on . . .

—Lauryn Hill

city of sorrows

Chicago is a city of sorrows:
let the 100 brown boys dead
raise up and tell you different.
Chicago will say it is the city
of the get down, city of grimy,
city of house music and hard work.
All that's true. All that means
is that Chicago won't tell you
how to fall in love. Chicago won't
give you back the chance to tell
that woman No. Chicago
hates you. When you're walking
the lakefront in July, Chicago says
nothing of the wind in February, nothing
of the terror of that cold when you're waiting
for the 78 bus. Chicago dyes its rivers
green. Sorrow. Green. The days
are proof of locusts everywhere.
This is not a metaphor. The locusts
are singing in the trees right this minute.
The whole city is biblical.
The whole city suffers plagues of things.
Ask the 100 brown boys dead.
And Chicago is trying to holler about Hull
and Algren and Kanye and Lou Rawls
and Jordan and William "the Refrigerator" Perry.
Chicago is a city of sorrows. Even the dead
Represent. Even the shot down
and reservationed Southsiders
will call out its name. Claim Emmett
Till and Dwayne Wade. Claim Studs
Terkel and four generations of Daleys.
Claim Irish America. Claim Italian America.
Claim Midwest heartland work ethic
and thick white women as beautiful

as a July 4th parade.
What you want Chicago? 100 brown
boys dead. Chicago is a city of sorrows.
Carl Sandburg and Ryne Sandberg both know this.
Ask any Mexican American claiming
West Side or Latin King trying to feed
a family of five. Ask them if Chicago
ever tells you how to forget the woman
you lost. Ask them when they're through
with their pierogis and tortas
and Harold's chicken how Chicago holds
Mississippi, Alabama, Tennessee.
Ask any Chicagoan where to go
when you wanna sing the blues,
where to go when you wanna cure
the blues, where you go when the blues
is the only work you can make.

how to write a love poem

Just today, telling a boy in county
how to write a love poem,
I'm stammering over ideas
of detail, trying to get him
not to say *happy*
or *sparkling eyes* but to talk
about what is his love's, only
hers, and no one else's
like how the first time
I picked up something from
somewhere, a book, maybe
a phone, and on the train platform
you smack it straight down
out of my hand and we stare
at each other dead-faced
for a millisecond and then bust
out laughing—*like that*, I tell
him and he's cracking up; he's
dying in this jail, where he doesn't
know how soon he'll be out
even though he's just eighteen
but right now he's full belly
doubled over and I describe it
to him again and who knows
what this beautiful, tethered young
man has done to forfeit his life
in this place but I remember
as he pounds the fused plastic
table how I want sometimes secretly
to hold your head in my hands again
and tell you that a castle of a brownstone
in Brooklyn is yours, that we'll
be sweet forever and make
outlandish things from fish and
peppers; and this time I'll mean
it, except I don't tell the boy that

part, but he only needs the part
where, when I least expect it,
you'll slap something out of my
hands and we'll roll on the floor
laughing and that's what I want
to remember if you'll remember
that too, except I worry you don't
but the boy tells me, still chuckling,
his eyes glassy, that he gets it. *I get
it*, he says; *detail, I get it, yeah*
and shows me the part he's already
written to his girl about how
he's not mad that a new man
is holding her and how she deserves
that because she is beautiful
and if he was the new dude, he'd
hold her too, and he respects dude
for knowing how deserving she is
and I say *Yeah, I get it, like that,
you're on it. You already know
what to do.*

Roger, Chicago, 2011, pens a note for his 9-year-old self, Winnipeg, 1977

(after Jimmy Santiago Baca)

You've had to leave your friends
so you will make new ones.
They have taken to calling you
outside of your name, so you will
become a stone.
They have isolated you amidst
a snarling sea of other,
so you will learn how to be alone.
They have attacked your body
so you have become a massive
windchime of fists.

Who is to tell you this is not love:
your mother's face, beautiful in its anguish
as she drives this strange city
to find you. And you are not lost
for hours, exploring these new sandlots,
and learn from their baseball games,
from their hard attempts to imagine you
invisible, that what is foreign and savage
is also gorgeous; in these short months,
you garnish from the harsh white winter
ways in which to stomp your feet in
demand of the ball, look white boys in the face,
skate like the hockey players,
befriend the tough Lakota girl,
compile manuals for living
amidst unspeakable hostility.

You have learned to be faster
than the other boys. You have

learned to lower your shoulder
and become a bull. You have learned
a slow-lidded callousness in which to crawl
before you bring blood to another body's
surface. You have learned the value
of your exposed ribcage, its alone
alone alone. You will turn
this into a spell song, into a plan
for fierce retribution. Everything
in you is already right and humming.

You will need to remember this
in the darkest of hours, even
with a blade gathering light
in your hands—
you are beautiful
you are beautiful

Simon and Lucy big up the sky

All children are my favorite,
the ones who know words beyond their years,
the ones who won't let me get away
with any explanation. *Why?* They ask
and, *how crazy is that?* Little Ames
in Brooklyn is 2. He can say the word
excavator. Simon is 7. He has discovered
molecules, but he is as yet incapable
of telling the difference between his black
and white friends. Here's the thing:
it doesn't occur to him to point
color out as a frame of reference.
Ames knows *yellow* and *red* and
Roger is the boy with the bicycle.
This week Lucy, 4, asks her mother,
are we white or black?
Her mother has known
this day was coming, when the world
we've made would come all the way
down on her children. I want to sit
and tell them who they are,
but more important, who they are
not. I want to say *Oscar Grant*
softly in their ears. I want to say
Emmett Till. I want to say *Saartjie*
Baartman. I want to say *Sean Bell.*

Lucy's poem to me says . . .
the ocean never saw sky. It says
the world never rose
like a rose shining in the sun.
Simon's says: a rooster crows
like a drunken horn. The next
day the sun rose and I know
little by little love leaks

out of us all through the mouths
of prophets.

Here's another: Simon cannot hear
of the poor. It makes him weep.
He wants to invent things
that will stop poverty. None of what
they learn to worship so far
is of this earth. They love me utterly.
They summon clouds, kites, the sun;
Lucy and Simon—they big up the sky.

Late summer—Chicago

At least the city warns you round late August
that it's entirely tired of your shit, your grand
summers of plenty and arrogance. You thought

you were going to learn the name of every
flower you passed on your way from the house
to the train. Not even time enough for that, for your gloat

of joy. *Look at the sky*, you told everyone. *Look at the trees.*
Look at the children frolicking in the park.
Now Chicago is about to bring everything

crashing down—you and your drum
circle of sunshine. First the wind;
and if you're not paying attention, you're thinking

how pleasant the weather's got—you're about
to praise God or some shit, not understanding
that it's his twin, beginning to laugh

across that massive lake. Still you go
out to the beach and marvel at the birds, the Queen
Anne's lace, the battalion of dragonflies droning

about. In this weather, the air is thinning and almost
cool, you're a blur down Wilson, up Kimball.
You turn onto Kedzie at such a tilt, you're Lance
Fucking Armstrong, the devil at your back laughing coyly.

◆

But you know, Chicago's weather will turn on you
like white people. Not even the wind is consistent
in its compass. Watch! it'll be no time

before the God of marigolds and dragonflies abandons
you. It's the time of the hawk and broken boilers.
Listen, the city's been trying to hip you to it since June.

The cicadas in the trees? God can't send enough
crows to silence their plague. They've been singing

since May. They know who their master is.
They've always known what's been coming.

a full 40 oz beer is tossed from a passing car and lands at my feet

and its roar is deafening—glass
and beer everywhere—night
and an incredible sadness
and Trayvon Martin is still
on everyone's lips
and I'm wearing a dark blue hoodie
and the people in the car can't know
what color I am or even
that I'm there—pushing
as I am on my bicycle
and I don't know many days
what the logarithms of rage
and so many people given
so much permission
to hate
       a man says *call me*
a racist but I couldn't care
as much about the character
because they made her black
which means
        America
has given him a history—too
and an unyielding right to count
my body expendable   When
did I become   less
mournable?   Who
mounted me such a mule—
whose death is unremarkable
for whom no one waits
at home as I pedal on through
the cloakish night which everyone knows
now after Sanford, Florida
adjudicates nothing in favor

of black bodies—which is to say
it is possible for my death
by mob to be so unremarkable
as to not be shocking
or newsworthy—my mother,
my woman should learn
to veil themselves in black
lace or shame
for even wanting me to star
in my own life—to return
home triumphant and drunk
with my God-given right
to the darkness and the streets
and this is what I pray
to sometimes—what is God-
given   what I know
is my burden tonight—is
Palm Sunday as I come
celebrated into the Calvary
of my own black history
expecting what the Father has laid
out for me—sure death by mob
who hurls invective and missile
who say black can't possibly
be rooted for—who will deny
who will say their hands
tied—who gets paid
for my death   every day
who knowing me already
convicted touches the hem
of my garment   says nothing
and is made
          whole

allegory of the house with no name
(for J. L.)

1.
You begin again, a fixture here,
your friends don't panic to find you
a derelict among broken playthings

muttering over and over to himself
in a moth-eaten bathrobe

and bare feet. How her name comes;
shows up uninvited to things—it's beautiful
really, you opine to no one in particular, again and again.

You remember the landscape of her,
how your hand wandered her nose, belly, hip,

knees, arch of shoulder, the half-pipe of her bottom;
and now the everyday hum of loss, how much time

you're spending staring at your hands—how they build,
how they break, how they build, how you called

her by her name twice—like a prayer.

2.
Your father's voice gets wearier from his half-
world away. You prepare your life to go

see him, and now you panic with the thought
of what you must bring. You've been preparing

to ask these questions all your adult life, but now
they're edged in something formal, ceremonial

as if they're part of the larger house you're gaining.
You need to inquire after this fucked up inheritance,

the stoic management of the heart, the body
convenes again and again. You want him to tell

you, from his massive bedroom, which takes up
an entire wing of his house, that it'll stop

hurting eventually—that alone will be fine,
a country ungoverned and secure; he's bequeathed

you quite enough to weather this life,
a quilt repeating its warp and weft into legacy.

3.
How do you ask about regret? How to broach the question of your
birth as if you don't know you're inquiring after his death? How do
you tell your gentle, laughing father that you're wondering about a
woman, as you ask him to tell history into the quiet whir of the
recorder? How will you tell him that you're looking for sanctuary?

4.
You're moving again. You've got better
at some things. You make budgets now.

You slow down enough to name things—
black-eyed susans, locusts, wind chimes,

the Chicago River, gardenias, dragonflies.
At the corner of Broadway and Bryn Mawr

you burst into tears, but you're a blur now,
pushing your bicycle through red lights

so fast, no one can tell it's you screaming down
Wilson until you're long past. This is where

you live now—Sacramento, Albany, Kedzie,
Kimball. You have to begin building something

so you wonder why not with her. Thank God
for your roommates. Thank God the house

is quiet just now. Thank God you can get drunk
in your room's squalor and not name your panic.

You do the safest thing you know: return
to the body—crunch and push up, stretch

and shadow box and hit the heavy bag until
calloused palms, your scarred ribs say no more,

no more. It is midnight. You look in the mirror.
The mirror says nothing.

You're dripping in sweat and the body is the only
control you own.

You're going to ask your father about music
and blood and your mother, the abandonment
of your infancy. You can

rewrite all this, but who're you kidding? All
you have is your body and its unreliable, scheming

heart. You know where the questions will take
you. There'll be a bottle of exquisite rum and

fried shark and a walk to the panyard. You'll
both be awash in the music. You'll both awake
and quietly go to what you both have learned to control—

side by side, running and lifting; bargaining
anew with death every morning. Funny

how you've developed these exact routines, a lifetime

away from each other, how you've made yourself
into your father even without him for example.

What will this sweet man tell you now?

Epilogue.
Remember? This was about a woman. This was about your hands,
how they keep building, how her name shows up, in everything.
You live there now. You've built a house with a faulty superintendent
of a heart. It's never had a name. The house is not your father's
fault. It isn't even yours. No one can live there but you.

Black Love—as told by my hands

I'm riffing on my hands, their sometime relationship
with drums. Trying to make them open and receiving, gift

of cornucopia, of prayer. What my hands hold;
babies and books. My hands hold promise

every day—of fist. There I go again, riffing on my fists
as if everything is a fight, as if everything is life

or invisibility, as if I mean to be black or something.
Often, my fists are promises. They hold daisies.

For the woman I love. They grip
my bicycle handles, my pen, a machete for the soft earth,
a butcher knife, to feed—the woman I love. Riffing on black

love again—like black love is complicated or something,
like it's even in the conversation when black love
is so often involved in loving not-black people, who then learn

about black love. What I'm saying is I went to see *that movie*
again. This week, *that movie* is called *The Help*. Sometimes

that movie is called *Driving Miss Daisy* or *I Can Do Bad All by
Myself*, which are also riffs on black love that involve
my riffing on my fists. What I'm saying is—I'm tired

of several black love narratives. Seems like there should be
several more. The one my fists conscripted for isn't difficult
or anything, but it does start in another country.

It does start with boy meets girl and they are black and beautiful
and it's the 60s, and they love books. Their narrative gets real

complex after that. The universal sign for grief and anguish is fists
pushed inward against one's own belly. Often I find myself

sitting like this for hours, calmly, like I'm made
of grief and anguish, like I'm black or something. You get me

don't you? Whoever you are, looking for love? For something
to count on? Often the woman I love doesn't. I try to bring flowers

or make food—mashed potatoes, rice and peas—trying to say things
grief and anguish won't let my body say. Sometimes we just
make love, over and over, until we aren't thinking about books

and earth and knives. Then my fists are hands again, holding gifts,
prayer; promising what they cannot protect—black love, babies, sto-
        ries, something
to count on.

for you who could know me who might love what I love

(after Reginald Dwayne Betts)

Love what i love—and know
me—loping down your block
    American Spirit dragging to a crackle—smiling
at babies—love your front lawn
and the Chicago spring tulips
    I stop to count—Pay
no attention to the shadow
of hood against my
face—I love Chaka Khan
Journey and Mozart
Love me—black and walking
    your block lean-to like
I mean it—love Biggie love
Nicki Minaj love pesto from scratch
and my ex-thug best friend's newborn baby
girl smiling asleep on my chest—
Do not say you do not know
    me—when I've been walking
your dreams all these years
    waving at your front porch
    asking in this fraternity of self-governance

Love what I love—a single
amaryllis shoot the give and
shudder of a woman's body—what
I give back to it—and know that
these things have saved me
have made me so
American
    and so black I can hardly
contain my joy—when

I see you coming and know
we can love this earth together
     the New York Yankees and samba
This is Al Green in my gigantic
Headphones—I'm thinking
of the hyacinths I've planted
in my mother's garden—Love
what I love—American women
and apple pie and Kanye West
and marathon views of the *Wire*
and black boys in hoodies

It is possible
despite what you've been told
to know me if you love
     what I love—children
screaming in an open fire hydrant
snow from inside a warm house
     Bustelo black coffee and
a good cigar—my fingers complaining
against a guitar string—I
am a man on fire
and in love—Stop me
and tell me about poems
your stint in the army
and Lebron   and that time you
met Gordie Howe in an airport
and you said something and he laughed
full-bellied and doubled over
Love me—love bourbon
Love Jesus and Brooklyn—love curry
Love Lucille Clifton's immaculately
husbanded rage—Love the places
I rest my head—I see
how you hold what you love
'64 Impalas and Independence Day
bunting and blondes and Elvis
and I will love them too

I love Muddy Waters and black women and Prince
I love Whitman and guns
I love Lil Wayne and orange gladioli—I want
you to see me and look in my eyes
and kiss me on both cheeks
and love
what I love—know me
I am a man—I'm an American
too

(for J.L.)

Cutlass and Garlic

Gulf

We crossed the gulf in a blue rowboat,
Hayden swimming the pitch blue seas
beside us. We whispered the count as we slid
the boats into the surf and roared it loud
as we hit the choppy Paria, the constellations
crisp as music in the skies above us
leaning into the water's weight with every
grunt—*stroke stroke stroke stroke*
the chant now a kind of prayer ecstatic
immersion of young boys into the black deep
on our way to the Guayagayare caves and
the deep cold pools inside them.

Start over. Once or twice when I was twelve
I dared enough to join the other boys
in theft of the boats so I could say I was there.
I was mortally afraid but grabbed
the oars and joined too in the shouting.
I wanted to be remembered, to be holy
there in the silent midnight waking
skulking quiet as ninjas into open ocean
braving jellyfish, drowning, and bigger
vessels just to belong, which is to say
I had not yet proven myself, and was
too afraid to decline the invitation.

We clambered over the limestone
to the top of the caves and jumped
through the hole one by one to fall thirty
feet through blackness to the unexpected
splash at the bottom. In time I'd come
to understand risk to be much like this
the heart rising through the throat
the body combed through and through
by an enveloping blackness every second
of the plunge a comfort of chanting

stars receding in a ring above
the body a boat   the silent pool beneath
a welcome death

The flagman has a vision

I does try to imagine
the ramajay, before is really
time to ramajay. In my backyard,
late in the night, especially
if it have a full moon, I like
to stretch out my arms
and just chip easy easy,
like I carrying a big mas'
like is Tuesday afternoon just after
a band come off the Savannah stage.
I singing the tune in my head.
I study how I will hold the flag
and make we colors
dance up Charlotte St. for every
body to see; how I will fancy-
dance the flagpole
like a sailor; how the women
will laugh when I give them waist
and bawl out, *Boy you is something
else, oui!*
      Sometimes when I close
my eyes though, I does see something else
coming—I see them boys from behind
the bridge coming, and you can't tell
if is pan or pooyah catching light
like that in the sun. Then I know,
I preparing for mas' and war.
But is nothing. My granny used
to say how that is all we ever
been getting ready for—if is mas'
is war—if is war, well then everybody
know is mas' in the place. And granny
used to go in the mourning ground
now and then and catch the power
and dance the orisha and them

and is granny who say to close
my eyes and see if I could catch
a glimpse of what coming for me.
        Me? I have a lawnmower
blade on a twine in a long pocket
what Mr. John from Back Street
sew inside my mas' pants pocket
for me. They can't catch me sleeping.
But you know what? Everybody
have to dead, so I waiting for that sign,
for the sign to know I going
but I not coming back. Granny say
I will know the sign when I see it,
.say it will come to me sure
as a Bible
say is up to me then to decide
if to go and play mas'
or wait in the yard for it to come.
But granny know me. I is blood.
She done know already,
whatever call, I going and meet it.
Whatever call I waking up early;
masquerade or warfare—is the same
thing. I in the fray. I going
and watch it—in the eye.

jasmine

My mother does not remember the jasmine
outside the window at the house on Mann,

the one with the 30-foot coconut tree in the yard,
how we came home, slid open the verandah doors,

and the bush, its white blossoms growing nearly through the lou-
    vers
and into the living room, would be an assault of scent.

How it filled up our living room with its funereal laughter,
how it out dueled the hibiscus for our attentions.

But it might be how that house's memories were for her,
the 1982 divorce decree, the quiet sitting at the table

earlier that year, in the morning sucking hard on a cigarette,
wincing with bruises at her temples and ribs,

how her hands ached, the knuckles swollen,
because she had accosted our father at his lover's house

and he tried to beat her, but rather found himself in a fistfight;
my mother turning over tables and lamps,

smashing anything she could, swinging like a woman
insulted by even the idea of being beaten by a man,

my mother who remembers only that her father refused to beat
    the girls,
insisted that her mother mete out such punishment

lest they become accustomed to violence at a man's hand;
though my mother laughs, it might have been the result

of his own failed attempt at spousal abuse, my grandmother
having collared him in her massive stone fists

and heaved him into a corner, so my mother could not be abused,
though we would all agree she'd been in a scrap that she lost.

So she can't remember that in that house,
where my father's lover dumped all his clothes on our front lawn,

jasmine bloomed all the time, and most violently so
at night. My mother can't recall the flowers,

though that morning, when I woke up and emerged
to hear her whimpering at the dining room table,

I could swear, through the smoke, she was staring right at them.

In the year of the cutlass

The cocoa hung low and golden
in the cool dark of the Tamana forests.
That year, I was taught
the specific English of the brushing cutlass;
the high arc you made with the long handle
down in front your left foot, the perpendicular
blade scything the brush into tiny green
tatters of rain with each deft rotation.
In the year of the cutlass, I learned
how to tell if the cocoa was ripe and where
to look for a snake in its branches,
for it was also the year of the *mapepire*,
the year of the *coral* and the year I first
noticed the cane being fired. I was taught
the cutlass would go straight through the thickest
cane if you cut down at an angle, in the shaft
on the bias and not at the tree's sweet joints.
I was taught the cutlass was a small spade
for turning the damp brown dirt to throw
seeds in, and then it could become
the year of tomatoes on the vine, the year
of pigeon peas and the year of chive.
My wrists became cabled and I could
trim the hedge bushes that year. I straightened
the ixoras and the hibiscus
with practiced, precise swings
that launched bits of branch and leaf.
I edged the lawn, needing
neither string to measure a level line
nor shoes to protect my feet.
It was the year of feeling sweat
and feeling my body bristle
like a horse's when the girls passed.
I learned the beautiful song
of the blade when it caught the occasional stone

and sparked shock up my arm. I learned
to aria with the blade's notes then,
how to sing in time,
every swing a metronome.
It was the year of the baritone,
year of the African sanctus and the negro
spiritual. It was the year my grandfather gave me
my own, its handle carved from cedar
with three rivets to hold the hard wood
steady against the steel. I learned
to let the water run the flat side down
the grooves in neat streams.
I learned you could threaten a man
with the cutlass and only beat him
with the flat side; the year
of the plan-ass and the year I learned
that Choonie called the blade a *pooyah*
and the peyol from Lopinot sometimes
called it a *machet*. It was the year
of rum and ole talk. It was the year
of learning to insult your friends
and the year of garlic on the blade
to make the inflicted wound
unhealable. My father left
and my grandfather started telling secrets
about who would come to take the land.
It was the year of practicing
to use the cutlass like a sword. It was the
year of sharpening my body.
It was the year of listening
to the different ways the blade sang;
the year of its tenderness against a fowl's neck
and the year of body against body
in the hot sun—It was the year
of lashing bamboo to make a table,
a small lean-to, a bench. It was the year
people began to die; and my father left
with the sound of a pomerac tree falling.

I learned to keep the cutlass leaned
by the bed, because it was the year
of the bandit and the shape shift,
plant yourself deep to come back
as something new—to learn slowly
how to leave so the cut is quick,
bloodless, barely burning.

Sneaking around on Death

War is what they called Anthony
in Carenage, when he was just fifteen.
V says Jackson closed his eyes and drove
the sweeping bends and dips of Sullivan
County. Anthony was gunned down eventually,
which is to say, before he turned 20. Jackson
died in a fire, lit by either an errant cigarette
or an unpaid drug dealer. For so long
it seems we call Death unto us by degrees
that no one is truly surprised to see us go.
Sooner or later, it is the reaper
who loves us most; or decided differently,
the one whom we beckon to hardest,
and who comes. At 18, 19, I pushed a car
into darkness' maw until it trembled
night and night again. Until now
Death is deaf, and I'm getting old,
tiptoeing around his back, hoping
all those calls I made to him don't
suddenly arrive on a fresh wind.
I've abandoned heights, sugar,
cigarettes, speed, fistfights, hoping
the relative whispers of drink
and lovemaking constitute nothing
so much as noise in the reaper's
ears. Today it is hot and rural.
I can hear birds, wind in trees,
and a creek running. Death
is the furthest away, even though
my glass sparkles gold with whiskey
and my heart worries so hard
over love that sometimes I believe
those laughing close to me can hear
its anxious searching for what is true

about what I've most recently lost.
I've bought cigars, new shoes,
a suit from a thrift store, and a baseball.
Renewal is on my mind—negotiation even.
I'm trying to forget the midnight sojourn
across the Gulf of Paria, the 30-foot dive
into the night pools of Guayagayare's caves,
the drunken night drives over
Maracas' cliffs. I'm hoping
Death doesn't translate them into
a too soon beckoning, because I have
this: Bob Marley encouraging *Live*
from a speaker, my body's muscular
trembling to run, my heart's insistence
that I might be on the precipice
of knowing everything
love wants of me.

Washington Heights, 1991

I got my A to my muthafuckin K
And I'm ready to trip
Slide on my banana clip

—Ice Cube

None of us was more than 5 feet 10
but that night we took on all comers
at the park up at the cloisters—full court
4 on 4; we played organized, broad;
our bodies one beast—loud
in the language of box-out, pivot,
run. Every rebound ours, every loose
ball won; every contest
at the edge of bravado and brawl. Afterwards,
when the dark determined us one day
older; after the other newly legal at drink
boys ambled back to their corners
or projects or parents' homes, we moved
deeper into the forest, brandishing 9mm
weapons. There, in the black, as our eyes
became more accustomed to the shapes,
we squeezed off rounds into the torsos
of old trees, loving the flat report
of the semiautomatics, the owls' hysterical
flight, the branches—so many arms flung
back into the night sky, wailing, so surprised—
at the power of the multi-armed God before it,
bellowing, recoiling; bellowing again.

In case you wake up in the morning and you're not in Brooklyn

Well. . . it's just that every day is a fending off, of a series of microaggressions

—Lauren Whitehead

You live in Chicago so you unfurl
your creaking body, brew coffee
the consistency of crushed coal
and slip into the first of several
layers you will need
against the Lake Michigan wind.

You live in Chicago and you're getting
on the train—you live
in Chicago and you're going South
Side. You live in Chicago, so you turn
your fitted dead straight no smooth
tilt to the front type; you make
sure you're not mistook
for set-claiming. You stay the safe
kinda black. You stay
scowl-worthy, your grill mean.

You'd better pray your body to the bass
in your fat headphones black because
you're going South Side and everything
here is black, is black and there is no time
for tender or to worry about the young
boy with the GD tattoo on his neck
across from you; no time to think
he could be your son and you love
this boy, and you want to ask him
why he isn't in school
and if he's eaten

145

but you can't do this because
he might already be plotting
to gank you, and you'd better
make him believe you're either
too O.G. or too not-give-a-fuck
for that to be a good idea. Still
you upnod stern stare every brother
whose eyes challenge yours, your
hat still straight-as-fuck black
though, because you haven't moved
so far from your mother's or grand-
mother's need to keep you
on a straight path.

And you're 6, and you get
a beating for not saying
good day to grown folks on the street—
for being rude—because black
and rude is throwback to black
and dead. And you're 40.
You drink after long days
of teaching in the jail
or Englewood or for the smug-faced
white fucking suburban New Trier
muthafuckas, whose earnest, ruddy
cheeks you also love. But you're black,
and South Side and your brim straight
and strong as that coffee you made
this morning. You love women
who are white and black and brown
and you are scared all the time,
so scared you memorize six ways
to throw the first punch.

Now you're a Brooklyn boy.
You've learned a swag for a different

time there. You are dap
in Bedford-Stuyvesant black.
You are Fulton Street barbershop
black. Malcolm X and Biggie
Smalls out either side of your mouth
black. But now, you are in Chicago.
You keep your fitted straight-narrow-
black. You're not going to die
today. You promised this. And
that too is black—the promise
I mean; the one you might not
be able to keep because your body
isn't really your own black
so you walk the streets
on ever ready. You're in the oldest
gig you know. Men with blues
in their brims keep time
on the headphones inside your head
and they're helping you keep it straight
on the red line on the South Side
today. You make your body
unbreachable. You're black, trying
to make it back to the North Side
which promises a separate gauntlet.
Your body is a constant negotiation
amongst power's several microagressions.
You're a hard brim. You're a straight
line. You made a promise
to your woman. You might could
love somebody. You might could
get home tonight.

Postscript

National Botanical Gardens, 1986

In the middle of the hurricane belt, hurricanes never seem to touch Trinidad. The meteorological maps are perplexed. They show storm after storm approaching the island and beating a path around it. Trinidadians don't even take precautions anymore. They prepare for things with "the gather" and "the cook." In Trinidad, we call it *liming*. Anything becomes a good enough pretense for a lime. Hurricane coming? Lime. Election results? Lime. The pope visiting? Lime. The queen? Lime. Armed overthrow of the government? Lime for days. It is the ethos of the Trinidadian. It is his magic. It is an imperative toward life in the same way Europeans know conquest. We are born in and reared by it. We believe it a God-ordained imperative: this mishmash of people from all over the world, all of us gathered here in this gateway between the Caribbean and South America, still not sure if we're here for good or if this is a way station, cannot be bothered by impending storm. We are a conglomeration of wandering tribes, after all. Our entire world is a marketplace; our inventions, of the show and beauty variety. We are supplicants to the make-and-give-away. We invented a thunder from the insides of discarded oil drums. We learned to bend wire into visions we could mistake for gods.

And with the rainy season almost upon us in August, with the thick, hot haze of the Atlantic always in the air, we're preparing to be gorgeous. I'm preparing to be gorgeous on a Friday night, because I'm 18 and I'm Trinidadian, and even if my job as a clerk at the Chocolate Factory says I have to come in that Saturday morning for inventory, there is no reason for me to not go to this party, to not lime all the way from off work on Friday, with only a brief stop back home for a shower and some food before I meet the fellas and we joyride all over the Northeast before we go to this big DJ clash, where everybody will be and besides everybody, Gail in particular, whose teeth are jewels in the calmer Caribbean sea to our west, whose smile is probably what calmed the winds that became gale force when they hit Grenada and St. Vincent and Jamaica, because no one as beautiful as she smiled at storms there. And there's no way I'm not meeting Gail there and holding her and swaying to some slow tunes in a dark corner right next to the big speaker box, my head a little bad with the rum and Coke I'm about to have.

So after work, I stop by Hereford's on the way home and fire a quick one with Uncle Mikey who is often there, but he's not yet drunk so he doesn't need me to carry him home, though he wants me to stay longer and have another. But I know it's going to be a long night and I intend to not be drunk when I see Gail, so I thump Uncle Mikey on the back and promise him I'll see him right there on that stool on Sunday night. And I drive home, slowly and easily for once, thinking of Gail the whole time and what I'm going to wear. I call the fellas, because you don't show up at no fete without your pardners, your boys. Dexter isn't coming out. Larry isn't coming out. Cyril isn't coming out, but Rudy is coming out and will meet me at my house and Dave will come out if I collect him, so I say yes. Because there's no way you don't go get your boys if they need you to go get them. It is the Trinidadian way. It is the way with your pardners, your number one crew of limers.

At home, Mummy has made a pelau. She and my stepfather are liming too. But they're staying in tonight. They are already divorced but maintain something between civility and passion. They are hurricane children too. This way is their prerogative. I lie on the couch and doze off because I'm tired a bit, and don't wake until Rudy's voice says *aye boy* from over the half-door of the kitchen. This is before crime makes it so we have to put metal bars on every doorway, before we have to think about home invasions. I startle awake to Rudy's massive shock of curly hair, and infectious always-giggling. This is before liver disease no one can diagnose for him. He suggests we should start it up right now and I tell him he knows where the rum is and he goes to the cabinet and pours the Vat 19 on some ice and offers a Good Night to my mother and stepfather while I go to shower.

I'm slower than usual in getting ready because I want to make sure to look smooth. I iron my best jeans, the Sergio Valentes: gray, skinny. Brand-new white Adidas with fat laces that my godmother sent from New York; my flyest plaid shirt, ironing it slowly, to Run DMC and Kool Moe Dee on my boom box. And when I pick my hair out and smooth down the sides, I'm ready for the biggest DJ clash of the year. I'm ready for Amitaph vs. C.I.N. I'm ready to hold Gail while something slow by Debarge comes through the big boxes.

Rudy and I jump into my mother's Datsun 120Y. I've had my boy next door Sean tune it up a little. Sean builds cars or modifies until they fly, so I like the little touches he can put on, how it leaps like a dolphin when I step on the gas. We take the back way, up through Maraval, through the Northern Range and the night, to go to Diego Martin to pick up Rudy's other pardner. We hustle along the black, narrow roads, me gearing down and accelerating through bends, for the thrill as much as trying to make up time. We stop at a snackette along the way and pick up three Carib, and I cradle the cold beer in my lap in between gear changes. We head back over the mountain after we pick up Rudy's boy. We head around the savannah, up over Lady Young Road, for the curves, for the hills and steep drops. We're going to get Dave, and when we pull up in front Dave's house on Pasea Main Road, he's waiting already out in front his father's rum shop. He has a bottle of Vat 19 in his hand, and he is easy in his slow leaned forward gait as he walks. Dave is still the captain of the West Indies youth squad. We still expect him to become an opener for West Indies within the next 5 years. Everything is golden in our expectations, because we are Trinidadians and the only time I've ever seen a hurricane was in 1974, and I came outside in it because no one thought it was too dangerous for a 6-year-old to go out onto the gallery to see the storm; because we're liming. Coconuts are bullets through the air, thrown from some massive invisible hand rifling the ball in from extra cover. Trees are javelins down Trinity Street, but miraculously no one's house is destroyed in our village. No one is killed. We liming, and now we're going to the DJ clash.

By the time we park and walking in it's midnight. We taking our time strolling in because we can't look too anxious. We can't look like we fighting it. We have to look like we belong, like is just so we move, cool, cool. I'm looking out for Gail, but trying not to look like I'm looking out for Gail. But then Gail steps out of the murky dark of the party and she's smiling that smile. She's wearing a matching burgundy floor-length skirt and halter top that sweeps up over her perfect collarbones and around her neck where it's tied. And her perfect belly is exposed down to where her skirt hangs onto her perfect hip bones, and she's smiling that smile, and I'm still playing it cool, because my pardners are meeting her for the first time and I can feel Rudy freeze with awe and Dave's laugh turn into a nervous giggle and as I remember it, Gail is even more cool and confident than I am. She walks up and slides her arms around my neck, kisses me gently on my mouth and I'm hoping that by the end of this night Gail will be my girlfriend, but it's early and the DJs haven't even let loose yet.

For a people absolutely unafraid of hurricanes, it's amazing how much we're always looking for rain. We can smell it coming. We don't want to be in it. We always want shelter from the rain, but it will not stop the lime. But it will stop us from going to work. It will make us late for any appointment. Like brown people all over the world, we see an appointment time as an hour before which we should not arrive. We see any appointment time as a sunrise. I'm thinking of this when I'm thinking how perfect this night is—even though I haven't heard from Curtis for the longest while—and I wonder about what time I should leave since the air is thick and it doesn't look like rain and I have a long day of counting barrels of peanuts and chocolate syrup and sacks of flour and candy-bar wrappers, beginning in about six hours. But I'm chilling with my fellas and the lime is sweet and there's a girl who is sweet and gorgeous and doesn't hold back when she's laughing so I decide that rather than leave early I'll compromise by not drinking anymore. So I go looking for Gail to get my hold and slow grind on, in the dark next to the big speaker box. Lionel Ritchie is singing *Hello, is it me you're looking for*, and clearly it's time, and when I find her, she's craning her neck to see where I am and smiles that smile again and we don't even have to talk, we just graft our bodies into each other's and I haven't yet bought my ticket to leave for New York, and New York is a place on television besides. Gail's neck smells clean like soap, like sunlight, like she washes in the river, which of course she does not, but that's how close my face is in her neck and how close we're grinding. Her fingertips are firm against my back and sometimes my neck, and I'm smelling something rich in her hair, and I'm not afraid of hurricanes and don't know enough to be afraid of snowstorms or tornadoes yet, and we dance through that song and the one right after it, without stopping like the beat was all the same because the DJ is on his game and knows how to mix one song right into the next so the couples in the dark don't have to stop, never have to stop being in love, because the DJs too know in their bellies something about a marketplace people who build temples of love out of wire and song and rain and burgundy skirts they sewed themselves, and by the time Gail and I get through the next slow jam, we know something made of carnival and hot sun and storms is happening between us, and I lean my forehead against hers and promise to call her the next day, and I stroll through the crowd until I see Rudy and Dave and make a signal in the air like an umpire signaling a home run, which means we're making a turn from there, and they should wrap up if they still want a lift home. And Rudy's boy decides to stay on, and my pardners decide to leave. It's a little past three when I step out the door, giving a fist bounce to some other fellas I see there, and we head home.

We're closest to Rudy, so over the mountains again; fast, the only way I know how to drive; the turns sharp. The roads are narrow, the drops off the road precipitous, but I'm not yet afraid of roller coasters or heights or failing or being in particular neighborhoods at the wrong time, or giving myself entirely to a woman whom I love. I drop Rudy off and fist bounce and Dave comes around to the front seat and we head for El Socorro and when Dave steps out the car and says *Laters* at about a quarter to four, I know I'm a little more tired than I would like and I have what is usually a half-hour drive home, but I know I can do it in twenty easy. The car is already ten years old. It has no radio and no seat belts, but the engine makes the car into a leopard and when I wind the windows down and begin singing out loud on my way home, I know I'll be fine. I begin with my choir's entire repertoire. I sing *Joshua fit the Battle of Jericho*, then I sing the *African Sanctus*, I sing Handel's *Requiem*. I'm making myself laugh by hitting *Wake Up Johnny* as I zoom past the Butler Highway, and the 120Y is doing 90 and I start in on the catalog of Air Supply and the songs of Bonnie Tyler. I'm singing Black Stalin as I hit the lighthouse and I know I'm almost home free and I'm singing *Bodyguard* from the Steel Pulse catalog as I gun up French Street, and nothing has ever happened to me. I'm invincible and my muscles still do everything I tell them to, so quickly I don't even have to tell them yet. I hit the savannah and I'm a genius, so I'm singing the J. Geils Band. I'm singing Michael Jackson. I take the corner by the College and I know I'm less than 5 minutes from home. I've done the dangerous thing and won again. I've beaten something and tomorrow I'm going to ask Gail if we can go out for real, to see a double feature at the cinema and maybe get some ice cream, and I'm pretty sure she's going to say yes and soon she'll be my girlfriend, and I'm damn near home, so I stop singing.

... • •

Later I'll say the last thing I saw was the Emperor Valley Zoo, which abuts the Botanical Gardens. Every day I walked to and from school through those gardens. It was a good long walk, about 30 minutes, and I'd dilly-dally going through there and get to school late and be in trouble often. And I'd take walks with girls I liked through there and steal kisses leaned up against the big cedar trees. Our cross-country race went through those gardens and up the hill at Mount Belvedere. So many of us spent so much living in those gardens, walking and jogging past the old historical ceme-tery and learning the Latin names of the bougainvillea and the poui and the hibiscus.

Later, a mechanic will say I was doing at least 80 when I hit the railings, but I know nothing of speed when I'm awakened by a hurricane of steel and glass. The car is in the air forever after it hits the curb and my ears are full of a gorgeous thunder. In the eye of that chaos, I can hear bullets of steel parts rifling past as I bury my head in my hands and abandon myself. I thank God I'm alone and for a moment I'm glad for the cocoon of the cockpit. The bottom of the car is grazing the ixora shrubs and everything is quiet, and I wonder where Curtis is again and glad he isn't with me, be-cause I don't yet know that he's been diagnosed with AIDS. I do not know he'll be dead in six months. Dave will be wheelchair bound in two years, all our dreams of his professional career gone, and I'm in wonder at the quiet still, and realize only then that I'm flying, and the 120Y lands in a thick patch of grass and in front of me, a massive beautiful cedar, but the car spins and spins and spins like a top, and eventually spends itself and stops. And I'm not even scared, I discover. I sit for a few seconds, and a se-curity guard from the nearby president's house runs over to see if I'm OK, and I tell him I'm good and the door can't open, so I climb out the open window and piss on the tire and walk back toward the street where a car has stopped, and they offer me a lift, which isn't far at all by now. I'm three minutes from home, and they stop because we don't yet know what car-jacking means in Trinidad. And I get home and wake my mother up and of course she's hysterical and I have to tell her a million times that I don't have the slightest scratch on me. And my stepdad puts his clothes on and makes a phone call and they get the car moved out of the gardens before daybreak, because Trinidad still operates based on whom you know can do what when, and it still does. And anyone on my block who sees the car with its broken front axle thinks I'm dead, because no one answers our door, because I've got up early and gone to work to inventory chocolates.

When I come home, I call Rudy and Dave to tell them what happened, and Rudy comes to my house immediately and together, and in silence, we walk down to where the car left the road and jumped the curb and became an airship, and we followed the flight and trajectory to where the car landed and made a crop circle of spins and stopped two feet in front of the tree that would surely have killed me, and Rudy whistles and scratches his head and we can barely talk except Rudy says *You lucky as fuck, Rog*, because we don't yet know how unlucky he is, that he'll be dead in less than ten years, his liver failed and failed and failed to keep up with the prerogative to lime that we hold as confirmation of our manhood, our Trinidadianness. And Gail never becomes my girlfriend because I never call her that day or the next and by the time we speak next, our moment is past, the way these things pass, easy like that in the blazing speed of youth.

My stepfather sent me for cigarettes in his car that afternoon, otherwise, he said, you'll never drive again. I trembled all the way to the store but came back safely, cruising slowly into our spot. I learned to drive fast again and I loved Marcia harder than I thought I loved Gail that night and we mourned Curtis together and made love again and again in the six months we had before I left home. But everything had changed. I knew something more was coming. I had to go out and make something happen for myself. I had to live at full throttle, even as I was more and more aware of how many storms were headed my way.

Acknowledgments

Poems in this collection have appeared previously in *Gulf Coast Literary Journal*, *Muzzle Online Literary Journal*, *Union Station Magazine*, *Louisville University Review*, and *Radius*.

Thanks to Haymarket Books, Anthony Arnove, and Sarah Macaraeg, and to Ruth Goring's and Dao Tran's editorial eye.

These poems and the venue of their making would not have been possible without Vox Ferus and its founders, Marty McConnell and Andi Strickland. They would not have been possible without Real Talk Avenue's co-conspirators, colleagues, friends, and roommates—in particular Emily Rose Kahn-Sheahan, Laura Swearingen-Steadwell, and Joseph W. Basilo. Chicago held me in this collection; and in that way *I can't never* stop thanking Young Chicago Authors and Louder Than a Bomb and all those young people who made much of my time in Chicago worth it. The young people in the Cook County Juvenile Temporary Detention Center have been massive inspirations even as they deal with a system, a city, an America that has failed them utterly. My employers there, the Free Write Jail Arts Program, and its founders, Ryan Keesling and Amanda Klonsky, are huge. My number one homie, editor, and sane-keeper and collaborator in Chicago, Kevin Coval, can't possibly understand how important he was/is.

The collaboration, support, love, friendship, and hard work in education of Missy Hughes can't be said enough of.

Marc Smith and the Uptown Poetry Slam's support cannot be overestimated.

Jordan LaSalle, you continue to inspire me. Your work and support and love have been invaluable. Thank you so very much for everything you continue to be.

Patricia Smith, Sean Thomas Dougherty, my brother, confidant, teacher, and friend Patrick Rosal, the louderARTS Project, which continues to hold New York for me, forever friend and support and collaborator Lynne Procope, Cave Canem massive, Queen's Royal College massive, Shonettia Monique, love in the universe for you always, Cara Brigandi and Grown Folks' Stories, Eric Williams and the Silver Room, Cheryl Reese, Krista Franklin, Avery R. Young, Malcolm London, the young people of Team Englewood slam, Kristiana Colon, First Wave 5th Cohort—R.I.P. John Vietnam, and love for all the folks whose names I missed, whom I love and cherish.

My Brooklyn blood family holds me tight—my mother, Hyacinth, my brother, Jamil, Shade, Simi, Olufemi, Femi, Wole, Ayanbi, Wally.

My father, Roosevelt Williams. Thank you man. Love.

Abigail, thank you and thank you and thank you so much—Love.

Lydia Merrill, mother of my child to be—love; here we go.

About the Author

Roger Bonair-Agard is a native of Trinidad and Tobago, a Cave Canem fellow, and author of *Tarnish and Masquerade* (Cypher Books, 2006) and *Gully* (Cypher Books/Peepal Tree Press, 2010). Cofounder and artistic director of New York City's louderARTS Project, Roger is also an MFA candidate at University of Southern Maine's Stonecoast Program. He is a consulting artist with Young Chicago Authors and teaches at Cook County Juvenile Temporary Detention Center. He is expecting his first child. He lives in Brooklyn, New York.